Department of Economic and Social Affairs

ST/ESA/264

AF863617

Measuring Changes in Consumption and Production Patterns

A Set of Indicators

United Nations
New York, 1998

NOTE

The designations employed and the presentation of the material in this publication do not imply the expression of any opinion whatsoever on the part of the Secretariat of the United Nations concerning the legal status of any country, territory, city or area or of its authorities, or concerning the delimitation of its frontiers.

UNITED NATIONS PUBLICATION

Sales No. E.98.II.A.3

ISBN 92-1-104483-9

Copyright © United Nations 1998
All rights reserved

FOREWORD

Indicators are essential tools for policy making, and since the publication of the Brundlandt report in 1987, policy makers and analysts have been trying to capture the concept of sustainable development in statistics. National policy makers around the world are trying to identify a set of indicators that would "indicate" the nation's prosperity, well-being and sustainability. Traditionally, the primary indicator for welfare and well-being is gross domestic product, in spite of general recognition that it has serious flaws.

The United Nations Commission on Sustainable Development (CSD) has established an international work program on indicators for sustainable development. An important element of this program is the identification of a core set of indicators for "changing consumption and production patterns" (Chapter 4 of Agenda 21). The set proposed in this report is provisional because it needs national testing, evaluation and further discussion, including discussion about what additional information should be available to policy makers and the general public concerning progress towards sustainability.

One of the challenges in indicator identification and development is to combine scientific analysis and public understanding. Policy making for sustainable development is a dynamic process that depends on stakeholder and public participation and support. Indicators for sustainable consumption and production need to be analytically robust but also simple, understandable and attractive to the general public. GDP has great communicative value, and it is this value that should be incorporated in a set of indicators for consumption and production patterns.

It is crucial that policy makers have key information about the environmental and social conditions of the nation, in addition to economic performance indicators. The set of indicators presented in this paper is only a first step. The Division for Sustainable Development looks forward to working with existing and new partners in the upcoming years to improve "measuring changes in consumption and production patterns".

Kenneth G. Ruffing
Officer-in-Charge
Division for Sustainable Development

ACKNOWLEDGMENTS

A variety of people have contributed to this activity of identifying a core set of indicators for changing consumption and production patterns (Chapter 4, Agenda 21). They certainly include the participants of our consultative round in 1997 and the workshop held in New York on 2-3 March 1998. The insights and suggestions of these over 75 people were instrumental in the whole process. It would be too much to mention you all here, but my many thanks go out to you, listed in the Annex 4 of the report. In addition, special thanks to Dianne Dillon-Ridgley for continuous encouragement and very able chairing of the workshop, and to Hillary Hillier and Bas de Leeuw for co-chairing the fruitful working group sessions.

Several colleagues, past and present, at the Division for Sustainable Development have supported the activity with suggestions, feed-back and co-operation. They include Joke Waller-Hunter, Ken Ruffing, Lowell Flanders, Ralph Chipman, Mary Pat Silveira, Jan Rotmans, Birgitte Bryld, Monica Luxem and Johan Kuylenstierna. Many special words of appreciation to Catherine Rubbens who has been the mainstay in delivering the core-set of indicators and this report. Many thanks to Lars Mortensen who was there when we needed him, and finally, the Danish Environmental Protection Agency for their financial support.

Erik Brandsma
New York, April 1998

TABLE OF CONTENTS

Page

EXECUTIVE SUMMARY

"Measuring Changes in Consumption and Production Patterns" is the outcome of consultations and a Workshop with policy makers and other experts working on changing consumption and production patterns and indicators of sustainable development. The objective of this process, facilitated by the Division for Sustainable Development, United Nations Department of Economic and Social Affairs (DSD/DESA), was to identify a core set of indicators for changing consumption and production patterns.

Since the Earth Summit in Rio de Janeiro in 1992, discussions on chapter 4 of Agenda 21, "Changing Consumption and Production Patterns", have focused on trends in consumption and production patterns and ways to influence these trends so that they become more sustainable. The issue covers various resource and policy sectors and has direct linkages with other important sustainable development issues, such as trade, finance, education, and technology transfer.

Changes in consumption and production patterns result from the choices and activities of a wide variety of actors including business and industry, households, and governments. The challenges faced by policy makers concerned with changing consumption and production patterns are to optimize resource use, to minimize negative environmental and social impacts of consumption and production patterns, and to stimulate and facilitate trends towards more sustainable patterns.

The availability and use of indicators for monitoring trends in consumption and production have become increasingly important in this policy making process. Indicators are essential for monitoring changes in the volume and intensity of resource use and the environmental effects thereof, and provide information about possible policies and other measures for changing consumption and production patterns.

This report distinguishes between two broad categories of indicators: "key resources" and "consumption clusters". It proposes various indicators for the "key resources", energy, materials, water, and land; and for the "consumption clusters", mobility, consumer goods and services, buildings and housekeeping, food, and recreation.

The distinction between key resources and consumption clusters is drawn, because it highlights the need for two different types of indicators: I) indicators of resource use and environmental impacts, and ii) indicators that reflect consumer and producer choices.

This report proposes a provisional core set of 17 indicators for changing for changing consumption and production patterns, covering all key resources and consumption clusters.

Core Set Indicators

For **Key Resources:**

- **Energy** (Annual energy consumption per capita, Intensity of energy use, Share of renewable energy in total energy consumption, Energy prices)
- **Materials** (Total material requirement, intensity of material use)
- **Water** (Intensity of water use)
- **Land** (Intensity of land use)

For **Consumption Clusters:**

- **Mobility** (Distance traveled per capita by mode of transport, Number of road vehicles)
- **Consumer goods and services** (Retail sales of selected goods per capita, Market share of more sustainably produced goods and services)
- **Buildings and house-keeping** (Residential energy and water use per household, Average household size)
- **Food** (Market share of more sustainably produced food)
- **Recreation** (Spending on recreation as share of disposable income, Time spent on leisure, paid and unpaid work, and traveling)

The selection of the core set indicators is based on the consultative process and on the use of selection criteria reflecting the consumption-production perspective and experience with indicator selection, definition, and use.

The selection of indicators also reflects a number of key issues that have been identified in the discussions on sustainable consumption and production, including eco-efficiency; cost internalisation; trends and developments in policy making; responsibilities of key actors; and the analysis of unsustainable consumption patterns and lifestyles.

In the selection process of the core set indicators, an effort has also been made to avoid overlap with other chapters of Agenda 21.

Governments from industrialized and developing countries and economies in transition can select, test, and use indicators voluntarily, based on national characteristics, needs, and priorities.

The core set of 17 indicators is a starting point for the further development of the indicators for consumption and production patterns. More work is needed for the development of operational definitions and methodological descriptions of the indicators. Furthermore, the policy relevance and data availability for the indicators will become clearer through testing of the indicators at the national level. The core set is therefore provisional, should evolve over time in a dynamic process, and should reflect changes in priorities related to policy making on sustainable consumption and production patterns.

1 OBJECTIVES AND CONTEXT

1.1 Introduction

This report is the outcome of a year long process of consultations with key actors concerned with "Changing Consumption and Production Patterns", as well as with indicator experts, on indicators that could best reflect the main issues and concerns related to changing consumption and production patterns. The process of consultations was concluded with a Workshop on Indicators for Changing Consumption and Production Patterns, hosted by the Division for Sustainable Development of the Department of Economic and Social Affairs (DSD/DESA) in New York on 2-3 March 1998.

The objective of the Workshop was to identify a provisional core set of indicators to measure changes in consumption and production patterns. Some forty experts from developed and developing countries, and economies in transition, participated in the Workshop, representing Governments, international organizations, the research and business communities and NGOs (ANNEX 4).

As the result of the workshop and previous consultations, this report forms the starting point for work on measuring changes in consumption and production patterns for policy development and implementation. The report identifies a provisional core set of indicators as a tool for policy makers in formulating policies and monitoring the effectiveness of policy implementation for changing consumption and production patterns.

The first chapter of the report includes a brief introduction to the objectives, context and process that have resulted in the selection of the provisional core set of indicators. The International Work Programme on Changing Consumption and Production Patterns, in which this activity is being undertaken, and the Work Programme on Indicators of Sustainable Development (WPISD) of the CSD, are also briefly reviewed.

The second chapter outlines key elements relating to changing consumption and production patterns. It includes comments on other factors relating to consumption and production patterns, policy strategies and targets, and trends and developments in policy making. It also reflects the discussions during the Workshop about possible indicators for changing consumption and production patterns.

Finally, the third chapter of this report contains information on approaches to indicator classification and use, selection criteria and the provisional core set of indicators for changing consumption and production patterns, including 17 indicators.

The primary intended users of the indicators are policy makers in governments at the national level. However, many other partners, such as local governments, NGOs, research institutes, business and industry, and international organizations, have contributed to the process and will have an interest in the findings and conclusions of this process.

The framework used to organize and present the indicators is the Driving Force-State-Response (DSR) framework of the WPISD. The indicators proposed are national in scope and intended for use primarily at the national level. However, the problems addressed are of local, national, transboundary and global nature.

The criteria used for selecting the provisional core set of indicators are the usefulness of the indicators for measuring changes in consumption and production patterns as well as the other criteria used in the WPISD.

The next steps will develop more precise definitions and methodological description, and examine measurability and data availability for the proposed indicators, and an assessment of compliance with the Bellagio principles[1]. Some of the indicators proposed can be used immediately, since methodologies and data are readily available. These indicators are already commonly used in a considerable number of countries, and widely accepted agreement exists with regard to their definition. However, some other indicators proposed in the provisional core set of indicators need to be elaborated further. More work is needed for finding precise and workable definitions for those indicators, and for developing methodologies for data collection.

The provisional core set of indicators for changing consumption and production patterns will serve as an input to the WPISD. Similar to the CSD indicators of sustainable development, the indicators for changing consumption and production patterns will require the development of methodological descriptions and testing by organizations and/or governments. If this can be done, the provisional core set of indicators for changing consumption and production patterns will be included in the revision of the CSD indicators of sustainable development in 1999-2000.

This report and the provisional core set indicators is also an element of the CSD International Work Programme on Consumption and Production Patterns and will be submitted to the Commission on Sustainable Development at its seventh session in 1999, during which chapter 4 of Agenda 21, "Changing Consumption and Production Patterns" will be reviewed comprehensively.

1.2 Agenda 21 and the International Work Programme on Changing Consumption and Production Patterns

Chapter 4 of Agenda 21, "Changing Consumption and Production Patterns" states that *"the major cause of the continued degradation of the global environment is the unsustainable pattern of consumption and production, particularly in industrialized countries"*.

Chapter 4, noting that consumption levels are very high in certain parts of the world, concludes: *"This results in excessive demands and unsustainable life-styles among the richer segments, which place immense stress on the environment. The poorer segments, meanwhile, are unable to meet food, health care, shelter, and educational needs"*.

Chapter 4 concludes, *"Changing consumption patterns will require a multi pronged strategy focusing on demand, meeting the basic needs for the poor, and reducing wastage and the use of finite resources in the production process"*.

Agenda 21 calls on developed countries to take the lead in promoting and achieving more sustainable consumption patterns. As developing nations follow development trajectories similar to those of the industrialized countries, it is essential that the latter demonstrate that resource-efficient, low-pollution production and consumption patterns are feasible and attractive. Furthermore, their efforts to move toward more sustainable consumption and production patterns should not hinder the development efforts of developing countries.

The broad policy objectives and related activities proposed in chapter 4 of Agenda 21, are presented in Box 1.

Box 1 Policy objectives and activities of chapter 4 of Agenda 21

In order to develop national policies and strategies encouraging changes in unsustainable consumption patterns, chapter 4 of Agenda 21 proposes the following broad objectives, to be aimed at by governments and other appropriate organizations:

- To promote efficiency in production processes and reduce wasteful consumption in the process of economic growth, taking into account the development needs of developing countries;
- To develop a domestic policy framework that will encourage a shift to more sustainable patterns of production and consumption; and
- To reinforce both values that encourage sustainable production and consumption patterns and policies that encourage the transfer of environmentally sound technologies to developing countries.

Chapter 4 recommends five major activities for reaching these objectives: (I) encouraging greater efficiency in the use of energy and resources; (ii) minimizing the generation of wastes; (iii) assisting individuals and households to make environmentally sound purchasing decisions; (iv) exercising leadership through government purchasing; and (v) moving towards environmentally sound pricing.

In line with Agenda 21, the International Work Programme on Changing Consumption and Production Patterns, adopted by the Commission on Sustainable Development at its third session[2], includes the following five elements:

i) Identifying the policy implications of projected trends in consumption and production patterns;

ii) Assessing the impact on developing countries, especially the least developed countries and small island developing States, of changes in consumption and production in developed countries;

iii) Evaluating the effectiveness of policy measures intended to change consumption and production patterns, such as command-and-control, economic and social instruments, and government procurement policies and guidelines;

iv) Eliciting time-bound voluntary commitment from countries to make measurable progress on those sustainable development goals that have an especially high priority at the national level; and

v) Revising the United Nations Guidelines for Consumer Protection.

The need for indicators for sustainable consumption and production patterns is clearly noted in chapter 4 of Agenda 21: "*Consideration should also be given to the present concepts of economic growth and the need for new concepts of wealth and prosperity which allow higher standards of living through changed life-styles and are less dependent on the Earth's finite resources and more in harmony with the Earth's carrying capacity. This should be reflected in the evolution of new systems of national accounts and other indicators of sustainable development*".

The CSD, at its 5th session called on the Secretariat and governments to *"Develop core indicators to monitor critical trends in consumption and production patterns, with industrialized countries taking the lead".* This request is also included in the Programme for the Further Implementation of Agenda 21, adopted by the General Assembly at its Nineteenth Special Session on 23-27 June 1997.

1.3 The Work Programme on Indicators of Sustainable Development

Chapter 40 of Agenda 21, "Information for Decision-making", calls for the development of indicators for sustainable development, and requests countries and international governmental and non-governmental organizations to develop the concept of indicators of sustainable development in order to identify such indicators (para 40.6).

In promoting the implementation of chapter 40 of Agenda 21, the Work Programme on Indicators of Sustainable Development (WPISD) was established at the third session of the CSD (1995)[3]. The overall objective of the Work Programme is to provide decision-makers at the national level with indicators of sustainable development. The aim is to agree on a workable set of indicators by the year 2000, through a process of feed-back and revision of the indicators. Indicators, as applied in national policies, may also be used for national reports to the Commission on Sustainable Development and other intergovernmental bodies.

Through collaboration among a large number of governments, intergovernmental and non-governmental organizations, a preliminary working list of 134 indicators of sustainable development has been identified and included in the Work Programme.

Several lead agencies developed methodology sheets for the indicators, including information on their policy relevance, methodological description and definitions, data availability, and the agencies involved in the development of each indicator[4]. An example of a methodology sheet, for the indicator "Annual energy consumption", is presented in ANNEX 1.

At its fourth Session, the Commission invited governments to test, develop, and use the indicators of sustainable development. The working list of indicators is currently being tested in 22 countries[5].

The WPISD recognizes that additional indicators may be needed to measure progress on some topics of Agenda 21. The indicators in the programme are intended as a "core list" to which other indicators, or sets of indicators covering particular aspects of sustainable development, may be added.

1.4 Indicators for changing consumption and production patterns

As a basis for decisions to promote changes in consumption and production patterns, information on conditions and trends of concern should be available to decision makers at all levels. Economic, social and environmental data concerning production and consumption patterns is available, in varying amounts and quality, in countries and organizations worldwide. However, the data is often at a level of detail that does not provide the decision-maker with aggregated information on the overall picture and the main issues of concern. Therefore, more aggregated information, as defined by a common set of core indicators for changing consumption and production patterns, is needed to facilitate decision-making for encouraging sustainable consumption and production patterns worldwide.

A set of 8 indicators for changing consumption and production patterns is included in the WPISD (see ANNEX 3). However, it was recognized that for this issue few suitable indicators exist, and that further indicators might be needed to address the issue of changing consumption and production patterns.

An Expert workshop on Methodologies for Indicators of Sustainable Development[6], held in Glen Cove, New York, 5-8 February 1996, recognized the need to further identify and develop indicators addressing the key issues for changing consumption and production patterns.

A background paper entitled "Measuring Changes in Consumption and Production Patterns" was prepared on the basis of a literature review of recent developments with respect to both consumption and production and indicator classification and design.

This paper was sent to policy makers and other experts in NGOs, business and industry, international organizations, and the academic community. In this "consultative round", the experts were asked to comment on the paper, including the proposed indicators, and to indicate what they consider the key indicators for changing consumption and production patterns.

Box 2 Objectives of the process

- To identify a provisional core set of indicators to monitor changes in consumption and production patterns;
- To initiate discussion and testing of the provisional set of indicators;
- To facilitate reporting to the CSD on progress in policy making for changing consumption and production patterns, and to contribute to the revision of Chapter 4 in 1999;
- To support the efforts of major groups to change consumption and production patterns;
- To contribute to the further development the Work Programme on Indicators of Sustainable Development of the Commission on Sustainable Development, and the revision of its indicators in 1999-2000;
- To contribute to the process of consistent national reporting on changing consumption and production patterns.

A revised background paper, based on results of the consultative round, and made available for the Workshop in March 1998, provided the basis for a Workshop discussion among policy makers and other interested partners on the identification of a core set of indicators for changing consumption and production patterns. The objectives of the above process are presented in Box 2.

2 KEY ELEMENTS RELATING TO CHANGING CONSUMPTION AND PRODUCTION PATTERNS

2.1 Introduction

The Earth Summit in Rio de Janeiro in 1992 recognized the causal link between current consumption patterns and lifestyles, particularly in industrialized countries, and major environmental problems.

There was concern over the climate change threat due to accumulation of greenhouse gases in the atmosphere, ozone depletion caused by CFC emissions, and acidification due to sulphur dioxide and nitrogen oxides. Biochemical cycles are threatened by excessive use of nitrogenous fertilizers and the accumulation of toxic heavy metals, radioactive wastes and long-lived halogenated chemicals in soils and sediments.

Other consumption and production related environmental problems are the depletion of fish stocks, forests, and water resources, the loss of agricultural land due to soil erosion and desertification, and extinction of plant and animal species.

The Rio Conference also noted the contrast between lifestyles in industrialized countries and those in poorer countries, and the inequitable distribution, both among and within countries, of the use of the world's natural resources and the generation of emissions and solid waste.

At the Rio Conference, questions were raised as to how consumption patterns and lifestyles in industrialized countries affect current and future consumption and production options in developing countries. There was also concern about whether the consumption patterns of the industrialized countries could be reproduced on a worldwide scale. It was generally agreed that responsibilities for improving environmental management were different for people driven by poverty to unsustainable consumption patterns as opposed to people whose wealth led to unsustainable consumption patterns. Concerns were also expressed regarding global dominance and dissemination of Western lifestyles around the globe, and the potentially far-reaching environmental consequences of such dissemination.

As the consumption and production issue encompasses a broad range of concepts, resource and policy sectors, and related issues (see ANNEX 2), it is difficult to find an overall and broadly accepted interpretation of all the elements covered by the topic.

Since the Rio Conference, efforts have been made by various countries (including Norway, the Republic of Korea, Netherlands, Brazil and Australia), international organizations (such as UNEP and OECD), major groups (business and industry, NGOs and the academic community) to clarify concepts, to strengthen our understanding of sustainable consumption and production, and to determine the responsibilities of various actors for changing consumption and production patterns.

The following working definition of **sustainable consumption**, which was adopted at the January 1994 "Oslo Symposium", is often used as a starting point: *"the use of services and related products which respond to basic needs and bring a better quality of life while minimizing the use of natural resources and toxic materials as well as the emissions of waste and pollutants over the life cycle of the service or product so as not to jeopardize the needs of future generations"*.

In the consultative round and the Workshop, many experts recognized that focusing on changing consumption patterns, while taking into account production processes, had the following added value:

- It promotes examination of consumer behavior that impedes sustainable development and ways to change such behavior;

- Consideration of consumption and production patterns together facilitates identification of the most effective and efficient policy instruments for addressing unsustainable patterns. It enables policy makers to examine simultaneously economic instruments and behavior-related social policies, such as information dissemination and eco-labeling;

- The sustainable consumption and production approach encourages all actors to optimize energy and material use, taking into account the impact of the use and disposal of products as well as resource extraction and production;

- The focus on changing consumption and production patterns encourages consideration of distributional aspects of these patterns, and encourages industrialized countries to take the lead in moving toward sustainable consumption and production patterns.

A core set of indicators for monitoring changes in consumption and production patterns, such as the set proposed in this paper, should reflect these factors, distinguishing the topic from other approaches to sustainable development.

Many policy measures, indicators and descriptions outlined in this paper will be particularly relevant for industrialized countries, since these countries are expected to take the lead in changing consumption and production patterns. However, the indicators should also be useful for developing countries and economies in transition, enabling them to track trends and shifts in consumption and production patterns and identify ways to change undesirable trends.

2.2 Other factors relating to consumption and production patterns

There are many factors and indicators of sustainable development that are related to consumption and production patterns. Many of these factors influence consumption and production patterns, many are influenced by these patterns, and for most of them, the causality works in both directions.

An example of a factor that influences consumption and production patterns is poverty. Low-income families are often driven to unproductive and environmentally-fragile areas, which they can only exploit in unsustainable ways in order to survive. They lack access to the capital, tools, services and training needed for sustainable agriculture in arid and semi-arid areas, in rainforests or in other areas with poor soils.

For the large majority of poor people in the world, the only affordable source of energy is fuelwood, which they must gather from public or common land in unsustainable ways, contributing to deforestation, erosion, land degradation and domestic air pollution.

Lack of access to education, sanitation, safe water and other public services further exacerbates poverty, leading to unsustainable production and consumption activities. The gendered nature of poverty, and other aspects of gendered activities and authority, are also important in determining consumption and production patterns and possibilities for changing them.

The Work Programme on Indicators of Sustainable Development (WPISD) contains, under combating poverty (chapter 3), a number of indicators of poverty, including indicators for the poverty rate, the poverty gap, the Gini index of income inequality and gender wage inequality. Under health (chapter 6) and education (chapter 36), there are indicators for sanitation, access to safe drinking water, school enrolment, gender inequality in education and other social factors.

Other issues relating poverty to sustainable consumption and production, especially in rural areas of developing countries, are covered under fragile ecosystems (chapters 12 and 13), sustainable agriculture (chapter 14), deforestation (chapter 11) and elsewhere.

Consumption and production patterns are also affected by movements of people, goods, capital and information. Rural-urban migration and international migration change the consumption patterns of the people involved, and often of their communities of origin. The consumption patterns of different areas and countries are also linked through trade and investment, especially direct investment by enterprises, which brings technology with it. Advertising, television, movies and other mass media, as well as tourism and other foreign travel also transmit consumption and production patterns around the world, particularly from developed to developing countries. All of these flows have been increasing rapidly in recent years as part of the process of globalization. Indicators relating to these factors are contained in the WPISD under international cooperation (chapter 2), demographics (chapter 5), technology transfer (chapter 34) and elsewhere.

Apart from being influenced by the above factors, consumption and production patterns in turn have an effect on a wide variety of issues. They affect the quality and availability of natural resources such as fresh water (chapter 18), land (chapters 10-14), and forests (chapter 11). They also influence health (chapter 6), the development of human settlements (chapter 7), and lead to the generation of waste (chapters 19-22).

The present report, while recognizing the effect of a wide range of factors and indicators on consumption and production patterns, will not try to cover the broad scope of the issue. Similarly, the report does not attempt to reflect the entire range of social, health, and environmental impacts of consumption and production patterns. In particular, those issues that are adequately covered under other chapters of Agenda 21, and for which indicators were already selected in the WPISD process, have not been repeated in the provisional core set of indicators for chapter 4.

2.3 Policy strategies and targets

An essential element of a strategy for achieving more sustainable consumption and production patterns is "eco-efficiency", pioneered by the World Business Council for Sustainable Development. The OECD defines eco-efficiency as: *"A management strategy based on quantitative input-output measures which seeks to maximize the productivity of energy and material inputs in order to reduce resource consumption and pollution/waste per unit of output, and to generate cost savings and competitive advantage"* [7].

Eco-efficiency strategies could also cover the maximization of the productivity of other resources, such as land and water.

At the OECD Rosendal Workshop[8] hosted by Norway, encouraging eco-efficiency was generally supported as a pragmatic strategy with potential political and economic appeal. Various efforts have been made to tie the eco-efficiency concept to specific targets. The "Factor 10 Club", a group from the academic and business community, argues that *"a political commitment to a tenfold increase in the average resource productivity"* in the industrialized countries is a prerequisite for achieving long-term sustainability. They suggest that the industrialized countries should aim at achieving a 50 per cent reduction in the global levels of non-renewable material flows over the next 30-50 years[9].

Box 3 Eco-efficiency

Increasing eco-efficiency means reducing resource use per unit of product or service or reducing resource use per unit of GDP. It does not necessarily imply a reduction of per capita resource use. The question remains, therefore, whether increasing eco-efficiency can lead to a reduction of per capita or total resource use.

A strategy for increasing eco-efficiency should include several sub-strategies, including industrial ecology, integrated life-cycle management (minimizing environmental impacts from "cradle to grave"), reduced energy-use, good house-keeping, dematerialization, and eco-design (See "OECD Workshop on Sustainable Production and Consumption: Clarifying the Concepts", Rosendal, Norway, 2-4 July 1995, Final Report).

Eco-efficiency emphasizes both environmental efficiency and economic efficiency (the "double dividend").

Some NGOs argue that a "sufficiency" strategy is needed to complement an eco-efficiency strategy. They argue that governments should not only set limits for various types of pollution and stimulate more resource-efficient patterns of consumption and production (eco-efficiency), but that they should also set limits to the total amount of natural resources consumed.

In a recent book on Factor Four[10], numerous examples are given of possibilities of many-fold increases in resource productivity, allowing more sustainable provision of the same service to the consumer without reducing utility or level of satisfaction.

Targets for increasing resource productivity are also noted in the Programme for the Further Implementation of Agenda 21[11] *"Action in this area should focus on promoting international and national programmes for energy and material efficiency with timetables for their implementation, as appropriate. In this regard, attention should be given to studies that propose to improve the efficiency of resource use, including consideration of a tenfold improvement in resource productivity in industrialized countries in the long term and a possible factor-four increase in industrialized countries in the next two to three decades. Further research is required to study the feasibility of these goals and the practical measures needed for their implementation. Industrialized countries will have a special responsibility, and must take the lead in this regard."*

However, the OECD states in a recent publication[12] that the concept of eco-efficiency does not offer a sufficiently comprehensive framework for determining which consumption trends are unsustainable and how changing those trends can best be managed.

The OECD argues that *"These qualifications to the value of eco-efficiency as a guiding framework for policy to change consumption and production patterns have two implications. First, a strategy of promoting eco-efficiency must be linked to explicit environmental quality objectives that identify any ecological constraints to consumption. Second, such a strategy must be transparently tied to policies to influence the other factors that determine consumption patterns and levels, including welfare and life-style considerations."*

Examples of concepts relating to ecological limits to consumption are environmental space, ecological rucksacks and footprints, and carrying capacity.

In traditional environmental policy making, targets for emission reductions are normally based on the capacity of the environment to absorb emissions to water, air, and soil, or to its capacity for providing non-renewable and renewable resources.

The environmental space concept was developed and applied by NGOs and research organizations (e.g. "Sustainable Netherlands and Europe" by Friends of the Earth and the Wuppertal Institute) to provide some quantitative approximation of the environmental impact of different consumption and production patterns (see Box 4).

Box 4 Environmental space

Environmental space is a normative concept with a physical and socio-economic dimension. In *physical* terms, environmental space is a measure of the capacity of the biosphere to support human activities. It can be defined as the quantity of energy, water, land, non-renewable raw materials and wood that can be used in a sustainable and equitable fashion. The environment is considered both as a waste-sink, absorbing emissions to water, atmosphere, and soil; and a source of services provided by non-renewable and renewable resources.

The *socio-economic* dimension of environmental space is based on equity principles, such as the idea that all people have a right to an equal level of resource use (intragenerational equity); and that future generations have a right to an equivalent supply of resources (intergenerational equity).

Some attempts were made to quantify the environmental space concept. For example, in the "Sustainable Europe" study, carried out by the Wuppertal Institute for Friends of the Earth International, the availability of environmental space per capita in the year 2050 was calculated for major resources, including total primary energy, timber, cement, iron, aluminum and chlorine. Assumptions were made with regard to the physical availability of these resources, the environmental effects of their exploitation, as well as the global, continental, and regional population in 2050. The calculations also included value judgements concerning the degree of environmental degradation or the risk the society would be willing to accept, and the obligations towards future generations ("Towards Sustainable Europe", Wuppertal Institute, January 1995).

Policy strategies and targets, whether they aim at emission reductions, productivity improvements, or limits to resource use, can affect both the selection of policy instruments for achieving sustainable consumption and production, and the selection of indicators for monitoring changes in consumption and production patterns.

In line with the eco-efficiency and resource productivity approaches, indicators should cover both levels of consumption and intensity of use of key resources such as energy, materials, water, and land. Indicators should reflect the use of these resources in a variety of sectors including consumer goods, recreation, transportation, or food production.

Increasing eco-efficiency, interpreted more broadly, can also be achieved by changes in lifestyles. Transportation, for example, could be achieved more efficiently if passengers shifted from private car use towards mass transit or car-pooling. An indicator such as the share of public transportation in total passenger miles, may be appropriate for monitoring such a shift.

2.4 Trends and developments in policy making

The core set of indicators is intended to provide a basis for monitoring the effectiveness of policies. Therefore, some recent trends in policy making for more sustainable consumption and production are briefly reviewed in this section.

In various areas such as energy, transport, waste generation, and water, demand-side measures aimed at reducing consumption have been implemented in various countries. Complementing more traditional approaches to environmental policy making, where the main objective was to minimize the environmental damage resulting from resource use, current policy approaches are increasingly directed at changing consumer demand and satisfying demand with less resource input and waste output.

One reason for the interest in this approach is that increases in the volume of consumption often overwhelm emission reductions through efficiency improvements (e.g. in the energy and transport sectors).

Another reason is that wastes associated with consumption now tend to exceed waste emissions from manufacturing processes. The effectiveness of policy making could therefore be enhanced by targeting consumers of gasoline, for example, in parallel with car producers.

Another key development underlying the selection of policy instruments for changing consumption and production patterns is a growing recognition of the need to internalize environmental costs. External costs (or externalities) arise when costs such as environmental degradation are not reflected in the prices of goods and services. Such external costs should be added to production costs, through taxes for example, and reflected in market prices, thus discouraging consumption of environmentally damaging goods and services.

Other factors such as the absence of well-defined property rights, environmentally harmful subsidies, and inefficient public investments are increasingly recognized as promoting unsustainable consumption and production patterns.

There are many examples of cost internalization measures, including reduction or elimination of agricultural fertilizer and pesticide subsidies. There are fewer success stories in the energy, transport, and water sectors. Substantial energy savings and reductions in environmental damage could be achieved by an increase in energy prices. As long as consumers do not pay the full costs of their energy use and its associated infrastructure, goods, and services, the development of more sustainable alternatives will be hindered.

Subsidized transport can be destructive to the environment and costly to the economy. When the use of private automobiles is subsidized directly or indirectly and when petrol is insufficiently taxed, private transportation soon crowds out public transportation and settlement patterns become more automobile dependent.

At present, the policy implementation process is largely characterized by self-regulation by consumers and the private sector. Governments determine policy targets, while other actors are responsible for the implementation of instruments for complying with these targets in accordance with their financial and institutional capacity. An example of such a policy instrument is a voluntary agreement between government agencies and private enterprises.

In designing policies for changing consumer behavior, there is a need for greater understanding of the motivations behind the behavior. Many policies used to change consumer behavior are found to be inadequate. Travel habits, for example, are constrained by a wide socio-cultural web of institutions and infrastructure, and measures targeted only at modifying individual behavior are not likely to succeed.

With regard to the transport sector, further social science research and analysis should be carried out to determine whether a "saturation" level exists for the travel activities of individuals, how telecommunications influence individuals' real and perceived travel options, and where the pressure points and "learning moments" are that enable policies to change behavior[13].

2.5 Indicators for key resources and associated environmental issues

The considerations of eco-efficiency and for delinking consumer satisfaction from resource use discussed in section 2.3 provide a basis for selecting indicators for monitoring changes in consumption and production patterns.

Consideration must be given, on the one hand, to the resources that should be used more sustainably ("Key Resources" - 2.5), and on the other hand, to the consumer "needs" or functions that should be satisfied through the use of these resources ("Consumption Clusters" - 2.6).

Policy makers concerned with policy development, implementation, and evaluation in the area of consumption and production patterns therefore need two categories of indicators: on the one hand, indicators that monitor trends in resource use and environmental impacts, and on the other hand indicators that reflect consumer behavior.

In this section, the use of key resources, including energy, materials, water and land, are considered in more detail. For each resource, indicators are suggested for monitoring use of those resources and for reflecting environmental effects caused by the use of the resources. Consumption clusters, including mobility, consumer goods and services, housing, food and recreation are discussed in section 2.6.

Where possible, mention is made of the type of policy target or strategy the indicator can monitor. If the indicator is part of the WPISD core set (see 1.3, 3.1, and ANNEX 3), the appropriate chapter of Agenda 21 is indicated. Links with other chapters covered by the WPISD are highlighted where appropriate.

Some of the indicators mentioned were selected by the Workshop for the core set on the basis of clearly defined selection criteria (3.2.1). The core set indicators are presented in an indicator framework (the Driving Force-State-Response framework), in section 3.2.2. For convenience, the core set indicators are already marked in bold in the following sections. Where possible, comments are also made with regard to short term, medium term, and long term data availability for the development of the core indicators.

The indicators proposed here should be considered as the key indicators covering the main elements of chapter 4 of Agenda 21, which can be the basis for a broader "hierarchy" of more detailed indicators.

2.5.1 Energy

While world energy production and consumption has continued to grow, annual growth rates have decreased, and the world's energy intensity (i.e. energy use per unit of production or GNP) has declined, particularly in OECD countries.

The main environmental concern associated with growing energy consumption, mostly of fossil fuels, is the continuing rise of atmospheric CO2 concentrations contributing to global warming. The industrialized countries today account for about 70 per cent of carbon dioxide emissions[14]. Industry accounts for a large part of global energy use (43% in 1992). Renewable energy sources provide a small proportion of total energy supply.

Five energy-intensive subsectors, accounting for roughly 45% of all industrial energy consumption, are iron and steel, chemicals, petroleum refining, pulp and paper, and cement. Other sectors which make a major contribution to energy consumption are agriculture, construction, and transport[15]. Recently, some new initiatives were undertaken by industry to develop indicators reflecting companies' contribution to global warming (Box 5).

Box 5 Global Warming Indicator

Recently, a tool has been developed by the British Imperial College and the insurance company National Provident Institution to help investors assess companies' contribution to climate change and their resulting exposure to financial risk. A "global warming indicator" enables companies to measure their output of carbon dioxide from fossil fuel consumption for making and transporting products or heating offices.

The indicator's sponsors hope that the indicator will become an internationally accepted reporting requirement in company accounts, to identify companies least able to curb their emissions and therefore susceptible to financial penalties. The indicator would also provide shareholders with more adequate information about exposure to new costs.

The indicator is being circulated to UK accountants and companies for review. Once the indicator has been reviewed by some of its potential users, it will be available for any business to try out, initially on a voluntary basis (Financial Times, 17 November 1997).

In developing countries, however, the lack of access to commercial energy often still is a severe constraint on social and economic development. Poverty and distance from supplies leave communities dependent on animal or human energy for labor and fuel-wood or animal dung for cooking and heating. Wood still provides up to 50 per cent of national energy needs in a number of Asian and sub-Saharan African countries[16]. In the last two decades, rapid expansion of the energy sector in developing countries has been accompanied by a decline in urban air quality, as well as serious land and water degradation from mineral exploitation and fuelwood harvesting[17]. Industrialized countries have taken the lead in pursuing energy-use reduction strategies.

Policy challenges are:

- Improving energy-efficiency in the production of goods and services, including within the energy sector itself;
- Increasing the share of energy from renewable resources;
- Reducing negative environmental impacts from energy use, including greenhouse gas emissions; and
- Promoting access to commercial energy to facilitate economic development in poor and rural communities.

Key indicators are:

Indicator	Comments
Annual energy consumption per capita (toe)	• Indicator for chapter 4 in the WPISD. • Increased energy consumption, particularly in industrialized countries, is a major contributor to global warming. However, the effects on global warming depend on the energy source. Therefore, the indicator can be broken down by source (e.g. coal, hydro, nuclear, fossil fuels, other renewables). • In developing countries, the lowest-income countries are often also those with the lowest per capita energy consumption, and social indicators such as infant mortality and life expectancy (included in the WPISD under chapter 6) improve with increased per capita income and energy consumption. • Focus is on primary energy. • Could be broken down by income groups. • Data should be available in the short term.

Intensity of energy use (toe/unit of production for selected sectors)	• Monitors energy use per unit of production/service. • Selected sectors will include agriculture, food processing, transport, and several other manufacturing and service sectors. • Can be used for measuring fulfilment of targets requiring Factor 4 or 10 energy productivity increases. • The WPISD includes the indicator Energy use in agriculture under chapter 14. • Data should be available in the short term.
Share of renewable energy in total energy consumption (%)	• Indicator for chapter 4 in the WPISD, formulated as Share of consumption of renewable energy resources. • Monitors the use of renewable energy sources. • Has an important communicative value. • Nuclear energy should not be considered as a renewable energy source. Fuelwood should be included in "renewables". • Data should be available in the short term.
Emissions of greenhouse gasses (annual emission levels in gigagrams of CO2 equivalents)	• Chapter 9 of the WPISD includes the indicator Emissions of greenhouse gasses (annual emission levels of carbon dioxide, methane, and nitrous oxide). • For monitoring the contribution of fossil fuels to global warming. The indicator can also be broken down by sector (e.g. industry, transport, agriculture, and construction), in order to identify priority policy targets. • An indicator of CO2 emissions per unit of primary energy can be used for approximating decarbonization.
Energy prices (US$ per unit of energy)	• In combination with disposable income, reflects the "affordability" of energy, for monitoring the extent to which energy becomes more or less costly over time. • The indicator also reflects the margins for price increases to influence consumption. • It is difficult to develop an indicator or meaningful proxy for monitoring the internalization of external costs, such as an indicator of energy price as percentage of full cost or share of energy tax over total energy price. Problems are data-availability and comparability among countries. • Data should be available in the short term.

2.5.2 Materials, material flows and waste

Despite rising levels of consumption of materials such as minerals, metals, chemical products, fertilizers, and industrial and construction materials, there is no short-term prospect of scarcity. Proven reserves of the majority of important metals and minerals, for example, have risen since 1970[18].

Materials intensity (materials required for constant economic output) has fallen in industrialized countries at nearly 2 per cent per year since 1971, mainly due to more efficient technologies and structural economic changes.

Though information about material flows is weak for most countries, the intensity of use of relatively unprocessed commodities (e.g. lumber, concrete, and iron) seems to have declined, with a shift towards materials with a higher value-added (aluminum, plastics, and composites). Moreover, the number of materials in circulation has increased dramatically. For example, an estimated 90,000 chemicals are now in commercial use.

The health and ecological effects of this large quantity and variety of materials are an increasing concern[19]. Once released into the environment, chemicals may combine with other chemicals to form new compounds, or degrade to other, potentially more harmful ones. Many pollutants, for example heavy metals, are persistent in the environment and can be stored in living tissue, accumulating in the food chain to highly toxic concentrations[20]. The consequences of releases of persistent or bioaccumulative toxic materials, heavy metals and persistent organic pollutants (POPs) are subject to increasing attention.

The volume of municipal wastes in OECD countries has grown from 347 million tonnes in 1980 to 484 million tonnes in 1995[21]. Changing consumer behavior (e.g. the shift to highly packaged convenience food), economic growth, and the increase of single-person households are chiefly responsible for this trend.

The amount of waste generated per capita in the OECD was 410 kg/capita in 1980 and 510 kg/capita in 1995. Figures show that about 1/2 - 2/3 of this amount is generated at the household level[22].

The per capita municipal waste generation in industrialized countries is about five times higher than that in developing countries, although the latter is expected to double in volume in the current decade[23]. With a few exceptions, OECD countries are now showing significant improvements in waste recycling, in spite of the relative weakness of markets for recycled products and the lack of reprocessing facilities.

In recent years, discussions about materials have focused on material flows and "throughputs". Various research institutes, including the Wuppertal Institute and the World Resources Institute, consider the total material flow as a measure of environmental disturbance. The reduction of material flows is therefore seen as a means for reducing the pressure of human activities on the global environment.

Efforts have also been made to distinguish material flows on the basis of criteria such as the spatial area affected by the flow and the potential for environmental harm[24].

Several measures for assessing the economic intensity of material flows have been developed. One such measure is the material input per unit service (MIPS), the material inputs necessary for the production, distribution, use, redistribution and disposal of a given good, considered with respect to the service provided to the end-user. Another is the cost per unit service (COPS). Both were developed by the Wuppertal Institute.

The World Resources Institute (WRI) developed, in cooperation with the Wuppertal Institute and several other organizations[25], a refinement of the MIPS, entitled the "Total Material Requirement (TMR)" of an industrial economy. The TMR measures the total use of natural resources that national economic activity requires.

Measures such as the GDP do not include the movement or processing of large quantities of materials that have no economic value. National economic accounts fail to capture many activities with environmental consequences, in part because the natural resources involved do not become commodities that are bought and sold. In the countries studied by the WRI (Germany, Japan, the Netherlands and the United States), the "hidden material flows" associated with extractive activities, harvesting of crops, construction and dredging make up 55 to 75 per cent of the TMR.

Policy challenges are:

- To decrease intensities of material use in production and consumption;
- To reduce the negative environmental and health effects of resource use; and
- To progressively dematerialize consumption - defined as a reduction of anthropogenic material flows, or as a reduction in per capita use of materials.

Important indicators are:

Indicator	**Comment**
Intensity of material use (tons/m3 per unit of production)	• Indicator for chapter 4 in the WPISD. • Monitors material use per unit of production/service (for selected sectors). • Can be used for measuring achievement of efficiency targets (e.g. Factor 4 or 10). • While interpreting this indicator, it should be noted that the mix of materials changes over time, so that the volume and impacts of these materials do not necessarily stay the same. • Data should be available in the short/medium term.

Production of heavy metals, toxic chemicals, and persistent organic pollutants (metric tons)	• For assessing fulfilment of targets for the reduction of the spread of dangerous and environmentally harmful substances. • Monitors possible future health effects due to POPs, toxic chemicals, and heavy metals. • Agenda 21 includes two chapters concerned with these issues: chapter 19 (environmentally sound management of toxic chemicals), and chapter 20 (environmentally sound management of hazardous wastes).
Generation of solid waste by sector (industry, agriculture, energy sector, households) (tons per capita per annum)	• For determining which sectors are major contributors to solid waste generation, and for monitoring compliance with solid waste reduction targets. • Chapter 21 of the WPISD includes other important indicators for monitoring waste volume and shifts in recycling and reuse of waste. Examples are: Waste recycling and reuse, Generation of industrial and municipal solid waste, and Household waste disposed per capita. • An alternative indicator for recycling and reuse of waste is Material input flows avoided through material recycling and reuse.
Total Material Requirement (TMR); annual flows per capita (metric tons per capita)	• Monitors total material input moved including the hidden or indirect material flows required for a national economy. • The TMR is an indicator for the "macro" level, and can therefore be calculated at the national level. • The TMR includes metals and industrial minerals, construction minerals, infrastructure excavation, renewables, and erosion. A considerable share of the TMR is occupied by fossil fuels in some countries. • TMR includes longer term investments in infrastructure and buildings, and therefore goes beyond "consumption". Special attention should be paid to the way such investments are treated. • Data should be available in the medium term.

2.5.3 Water

Worldwide water use is increasing steadily, and has nearly doubled since 1960. Annual withdrawals reached a level of 4,138 km3 in 1990. Per capita availability of freshwater worldwide fell from 17,000 m3 in 1950 to 7,300 m3 in 1995, primarily as a result of population growth[26]. In developing countries, 70 to 90 per cent of water use is for agriculture, against 39 per cent in developed countries. Water use for industry and domestic consumption are considerably higher in high-income countries[27].

There is heavy overuse of groundwater in a number of regions, with water being pumped out faster than nature replenishes the stock. Overpumping of groundwater has lowered water levels by tens of meters in some places, making it increasingly difficult and expensive to pump more water. Overuse of groundwater can have a serious effect on river flows, and can result in sinking land above aquifers and lead to intrusion of salt water into aquifers near coasts[28].

Rivers, lakes, oceans, and underground aquifers are used as waste-sinks. Water pollution originates from various sources, including untreated sewage, chemical discharges, petroleum leaks and spills, dumping in old mines and pits, and agricultural chemicals[29]. In many areas, waste discharge has outstripped nature's capacity to break down wastes into less harmful elements, adversely affecting water quality and posing risks to human health.

One billion people in developing countries still lack access to adequate water supply, while 1.7 billion people lack adequate sanitation facilities[30].

Finally, water resources also host fish resources (Box 6), the supply of which crucially depends on water quality and quantity.

Box 6 The role of Fish in the world's food supply

Marine and inland fish resources are an important component of the world's food supply. About 950 million people, mostly in developing countries, rely on fish for their primary source of protein. The marine catch (representing about 78 per cent of the total) rose nearly five-fold between 1950 and 1989. It has dropped slightly since then, but the total catch has continued to rise thanks to expanded aquaculture production. According to a recent study, about 35 per cent of the world's major fisheries now have declining yields, about 25 per cent are at high levels of exploitation, and 40 per cent still have a potential for yield increase.

The main concerns in the fisheries sector are fish depletion and species extinction because of over exploitation, inappropriate fishing methods, water pollution and the construction of dams. Aquaculture can also cause environmental problems, such as salinization, pollution of ground and surface water, and mangrove depletion.

Policy challenges are:

- An integrated approach to water policy making, including quality issues (i.e. to reduce pollution of water resources, contributing to a solution of the water scarcity problem) and quantity issues (so that the lack of water does not become a major constraint on development);

- To improve the efficiency of water use in the agricultural sector (particularly through improved irrigation techniques and management), industry, and households;

- To allocate water more rationally among users; and

- To avoid depletion of fish stocks.

Key indicators are:

Indicator	Comment
Annual withdrawals of ground and surface water (as % of available water supply)[31]	• Indicator for chapter 18 in the WPISD.
Water availability per capita (m3 per year)	• Currently, no internationally agreed definition of water availability exists. • Water availability per capita can vary from one region to another, and is therefore of less relevance at the national level. The significance of the indicator would be increased, if disaggregated by regions, such as watersheds. • Indicator can be related to indicators for water demand per capita and for water supply per capita.
Intensity of water use (m3 per unit of production)	• Monitors efficiency of water use for selected sectors (e.g. several industrial and services sectors). • In using the above indicator of annual withdrawals of ground and surface water as percentage of available water supply (particularly if disaggregated locally), one can decide if the intensity of water use of particular sectors is sustainable, and identify priority sectors for water conservation (given country-specific characteristics such as financial coping capability[32]). • Indicator for residential water use per household is included under buildings and housekeeping. • Can be used for measuring achievement of targets requiring quantified water productivity increases. • Data should be available in the short term.
Sectoral contribution to water pollution (nutrients) (industry, agriculture, households) (per capita)	• Indicator for determining major contributors to water pollution.
Access to safe drinking water (% of population)	• Indicator for chapter 6 in the WPISD. • Approximation of the potential for health effects due to polluted drinking water.

Stock of marine species relative to stock for maximum sustainable yield (%)	• Indicator for chapter 17 in the WPISD.

2.5.4 Land

Land resources contribute not only to agricultural and forest production, but also to renewable energy and biodiversity stocks and water resources. Both the quantity and quality of land resources are important as a measure of the ability of land resources to fulfil economic, social and ecological functions[33].

One of the important functions of land is to ensure food security, a function that is threatened by shifts in land use towards urbanization, infrastructure, and the provision of non-food products and services (e.g. recreation, paper, fibers, biomass energy); and by unsustainable agricultural practices. Land is an increasingly scarce resource, fulfilling a large variety and an increasing number of vital and competing functions.

At present, slightly less than 1.5 billion ha of arable land is in use, currently about 0.28 ha per capita[34]. Each year, an estimated 0.5 to 1 percent of arable land is lost due to desertification, erosion, or salinization and once degraded, soil is often impossible to rehabilitate.

Demand for food production has led to a steady increase in cropland. By the early 1990's, almost 40 per cent of the Earth's land surface had been converted to cropland and permanent pasture, largely at the expense of forests and natural grassland. The most dramatic changes are occurring in developing countries, where it is estimated that from 1960 to 1990, one fifth of all natural tropical forest was cleared for cultivation.

Agricultural practices can cause a wide variety of environmental problems, depending on geographical factors, soil type, and the scale or intensity of the activity. Intensified agriculture can result in pesticide and fertilizer contamination, soil erosion, soil and water pollution, and biodiversity loss.

Conversion of land from forest to agriculture is expected to continue: recent estimates suggest that nearly two thirds of tropical deforestation - some 12 million hectares per year - is due to farmers clearing land for agriculture[35]. Deforestation is a major threat, since forests are not only an important source of goods and services, but also valuable as regulators of global climate, as repositories of species, and as protectors of soil and water resources.

In 1990, forests and other wooded land covered 5.1 billion ha, about 40 per cent of the earth's land area. Between 1980 and 1990, the world's forest and other wooded land area declined by 2 per cent - or 100 million hectares[36].

Box 7 Ecological Footprint

In order to illustrate the unequal worldwide consumption of the goods and services deriving from land resources, Rees and Wackernagel (1994) developed the concept of the "Ecological Footprint". The latter can be defined as the area of land required by a given group of people (household, city, or country) to provide the goods and services it consumes, and to assimilate its waste products, wherever that land may be located.

For example, it was reported by researchers that the aggregate consumption of wood, paper, fibre, and food by the inhabitants of 29 cities in the Baltic Sea drainage basin appropriated an ecosystem area 200 times larger than the cities themselves. In another study, it was estimated that London's ecological footprint for food, forest products, and carbon assimilation occupied 120 times the surface area of the city proper (Rees, "Reducing the Ecological Footprint of Consumption", 1995).

Policy challenges are:

- To maximize the productive uses of land, including provision of renewable and non-renewable resources, urban space, industrial estates, infrastructure, critical natural ecosystems and recreation, with multiple uses where possible;
- To halt and reverse land degradation due to erosion, desertification, salinization, deforestation, and other causes;
- To reduce environmental damage due to intensified agricultural practices; and
- To establish stronger links between land use planning policies and other policies.

Possible indicators are:

Indicator	**Comment**
Land use (per capita and as % of total land area)	• Monitors land use (including forestry, agriculture, settlements, infrastructure, recreation), and changes in land use patterns. • Strong links exist with the transport sector, in particular in the area of spatial planning for transportation infrastructure in urban areas (see 2.6.1). • Data should be available in the short term.

Land use change (% change of each category of land use to another land use per unit of time)	• Indicator for chapter 10 in the WPISD. • The above indicator, if measured at different time intervals, will provide similar information.
Changes in land conditions (the extent and magnitude of improvement and deterioration in land condition changes)	• Indicator for chapter 10 in the WPISD. • Changes are disaggregated by type and geographic location, and in the condition, suitability, and nature of the land resource. • Strong links exist with the transport sector, in particular in relation to increases in fragmented areas and impervious surfaces (see 2.6.1).

2.6 Indicators for consumption clusters

In order to develop and implement the most effective policies for making consumption and production patterns more sustainable, policy makers need to know why and how consumers and producers make choices and decisions. Understanding these decision making processes will indicate the most effective leverage points for policy design. In combination with information on resource use, data on how consumers and producers fulfil needs and functions is essential.

Consumers can find various ways to fulfil their needs. The need for mobility or access, for example, can be satisfied by taking a bus, a train, private car, bicycle, or by walking. The demand for communication can be satisfied, in some cases, by taking these modes of transportation (thereby also satisfying the demand for mobility), but also by means of a telephone call, or by sending a message through electronic mail.

As mentioned in section 2.4, policy makers have become more interested in the motivations behind consumer behavior, such as saving time, saving money, following fashion trends, or enjoying life. These motivations, however, are difficult to measure. Several "consumption clusters" are considered here, with consumer "needs" and functions as a basis. The clusters selected include mobility, consumer goods and services, buildings and housekeeping, food, and recreation.

While comments are made for each cluster with regard to possible motivations behind current consumption trends, the focus is on measurable aspects of these trends and on the potential for changing to more sustainable consumption patterns ("lifestyles"), without reducing the satisfaction or quality of life of the consumer.

The indicators listed under the consumption clusters reflect current consumption patterns, their main direct or indirect effects on resource use and the environment, and indications of shifts in these patterns towards more sustainable ones.

Sometimes, more sustainable consumption patterns can be achieved through a shift to communal activities or from buying products to services (e.g. the use of public transport instead of private cars, or the use of a laundry service instead of buying a washing-machine). Alternatively, a consumer can choose a good or service produced or provided in a more sustainable manner than a competing product or service on the basis of an eco-label. A recent UN report, "Unlocking Trade Opportunities", illustrates this with case studies, in particular where developing country producers have been able to benefit from new export opportunities[37]. Consumers, producers, and the retail sector can also enhance sustainable consumption by extending product life, and reducing resource waste through increased use of product repair and exchange services[38].

2.6.1 Mobility

Motor vehicle stocks increased by about 50 per cent in OECD countries over the period 1980-1995, while the worldwide increase has amounted to 57 per cent. The number of passenger cars in use increased by about 47 per cent in OECD countries, and road traffic volumes (of motor vehicles) increased by about 84 per cent over the same period of time[39]. Vehicle stocks have also increased in many developing countries. In China, for example, the number of passenger vehicles almost tripled between 1988 and 1994, and the number of trucks increased by 76 per cent over the same period[40]. Between 1960 and 1990, world wide air transport increased ten-fold, and the sector is still rapidly growing[41]. Current trends also show that the energy intensity in the transportation sector is increasing, especially due to increasing use of planes, high-speed trains, and larger and heavier vehicles.

Energy consumption and CO2 emissions are among the most serious of the many traffic-induced environmental problems. The sector also contributes substantially to other types of air pollution, particularly nitrogen oxides, sulphur dioxide, volatile organic compounds, small particles and smog. The extent to which the transportation sector contributes to air pollution depends on the size, type, and efficiency of the vehicles used. The sector can also have important effects on the quality of life, for example, through the generation of noise, congestion and accidents. As was mentioned in section 2.5.4, increased traffic and transport infrastructure can also strongly affect land quality and land use, e.g. through the fragmentation of land and increases in impervious land surfaces.

In the transport sector, energy efficiency gains are being offset by volume increases. Technological developments, such as catalyc converters or improved energy efficiency, have are not been sufficient to reduce environmental damage arising from transportation.

Land use planning, combined with regulatory, social, and pricing measures, including transport prices that also reflect environmental and social costs, are necessary to move toward more sustainable transportation systems.

The car represents more than merely a means of transport. For some, car ownership reflects social status, for others, a sense of freedom or privacy. Motivations behind the choice of taking the car rather than using public transport are also more complex than simply the need for mobility, or the price of gasoline as compared to the price of a bus- or train-ticket. More knowledge about the complex reasons underlying transport behavior is needed for policy making in the transportation sector.

In the era of the "information super highway", new means of communication and an improved communication and information infrastructure can affect the use of transportation. Activities such as teleworking, teleconferencing, teleselling and teleshopping, for example, can reduce the need for mobility. Rapid developments in this area may well benefit policy making targeted at reducing the environmental impacts of mobility. However, increased communication also appears to stimulate increased travel for business and leisure. The identification of the consequences of information technologies deserves increasing attention.

Another important aspect of transportation that is important for changing consumption and production patterns (particularly of food and consumer goods) is freight transport. The shipment of products or commodities over very long distances for processing, assembly, and distribution is not efficient from an environmental perspective. Further work in this area is needed to address the key freight issues for policy makers (e.g. the price of gasoline).

Policy challenges are:

- To shift towards more energy and material efficient technologies and practices in the transport sector through spatial planning, urban design, and by enhancing the capacity of existing infrastructure;
- To reduce the need for travel and transport; and
- To increase understanding of the motivations behind choices of means of transportation.

Agenda 21 has no chapter on transport. As a result, the WPISD only includes one indicator directly related to the sector (Per capita consumption of fossil fuel by motor vehicle transport, under chapter 7).

Therefore, discussions on indicators for chapter 4 provide an opportunity to consider indicators for transport, in particular those that concern travel behavior. In selecting additional indicators for the transport sector, attention should be given to the considerable work that was already carried out in this area, both at the national level and through international organizations.

The most important mobility related indicators for decision makers are concerned with travel mode (including fuel-efficiency, size, and environmental impact of types of vehicles), distance traveled, frequency of travel, and the time individuals spend traveling.

Important indicators are:

Indicator	**Comment**
Number of road vehicles (total and per capita)	• Monitors the total number of vehicles, and motorization. • The indicator should be broken down into types of vehicles, and into categories reflecting fuel-efficiency of vehicles (gas-mileage). Vehicles could also be classified on the basis of atmospheric emissions generated. • OECD indicator for the integration of environmental concerns into transport policies. • Data should be available in the short term.
Distance traveled per capita by mode of transport (km)	• Monitors the use of different modes of transport (foot, bicycle, train, boat, car, bus, plane). • More detailed indicators for monitoring transport are: Average distance from home to super-markets, Average distance home-work, or Average distance traveled from home to collect fuelwood. These indicators should include indicators for frequency of travel and voluntary trips as opposed to necessary trips. • Data should be available in the short/medium term.
Atmospheric emissions of pollutants from the transport sector (tonnes per unit of GDP or per capita)	• Indicator used by the OECD. • For monitoring compliance with CO2, NOx, and VOC reduction objectives.
Freight traffic by mode of transport (tonne-km per capita)	• Monitors freight volume and reflects environmental impact. • Total volume and changes in freight traffic by mode of transport are directly linked to energy price, geography, and infrastructure. However, international freight traffic may be difficult to address at the national level under the umbrella of "changing consumption and production patterns".

Per capita consumption of fossil fuel by motor vehicle transport (liters)	•	Indicator for chapter 7 in the WPISD.
Fuel price taxation (by fuel type) (% of fuel price)	• •	Indicates extent of cost internalization in the transport sector. Other policy indicators relating to mobility are: Subsidies for public transport, and Ratio of public to private public transport in urban areas.
Number of computers per 1000 inhabitants and/or connections to the internet	•	Monitors the potential for electronic communication. However, while computer use can in theory replace travel, empirical evidence confirming this is currently lacking. Further work on the impacts of factors such as telecommuting and electronic commerce is needed.

2.6.2 Consumer goods and services

Consumers need and want goods and services for eating, cleaning, dressing, home decorating, leisure activities and for numerous other purposes. The choice of replacing an old product by a new one can be made because the old product cannot be repaired or reused, for reasons of aesthetics or fashion, for convenience, or because the product is considered obsolete from a technical standpoint. Consumer goods and services, and trends in their production, delivery, design, durability, and disposal are a major factor in sustainable development in both the developed and developing world.

Goods purchased by consumers range from tools and appliances, clothing and footwear, and toiletries, to cosmetics, books, and furniture. In 1993, world wide production of shoes amounted to about 4 billion pairs, that of bed linen to about 700 million units, and that of washing powders and detergents to 13 million metric tons. In the same year, the worldwide production of hardware was estimated at about 750.000 metric tons, that of sewing machines at 15 million units, and that of washing machines for household use to about 45 million units[42]. Production volumes of most consumer goods are increasing. The annual growth in the world production of refrigerators for household use, for example, was 3.4 percent from 1984-1993, and of fabrics 2.8 per cent.

Consumers directly and indirectly contribute to environmental effects throughout a product's life-cycle. Direct energy consumption is particularly high for products for lighting, heating and cooling homes, and for cooking and storing food. In many OECD countries, the number of products using electricity in the household is still rising, and consumers increasingly buy both second pieces of equipment (e.g. a second television set) and new types of products they did not own before (e.g. micro-wave ovens)[43].

Another consumer good involving direct consumer impacts on the environment in the use and disposal phases, and indirectly in the production phase, is paper. The pulp and paper industry is not only the major worldwide consumer of wood (the industry uses roughly one third of the global industrial wood harvest - excluding fuelwood), but it ranks third in terms of financial turnover and in the top 10 industries that emit greenhouse gasses (carbon dioxide and methane). Moreover, when paper is bleached with chlorine gas, highly toxic dioxins can be released into the environment (Box 8).

Box 8 Distribution of Paper Use

Paper use reflects economic development. Current paper consumption (1993) in developed countries is 152 kg per person per year, and in developing countries only 12 kg per person per year. The amount of paper used reflects demand for paper for reading and writing, especially in developing countries. More than a billion adults are still illiterate and over 100 million children worldwide receive no primary education. The demand for pulpwood for paper is expected to double in the next 50 years (WBCSD, "A Changing Future for Paper," 1996).

Media and advertising have an important impact on the purchase of goods and services[44]. Advertising in particular strongly affects motivations underlying consumption trends and therefore plays an important role in shaping consumption and production patterns.

Several studies indicate that consumption and production patterns can be made more sustainable by substituting certain services for goods with the same function fulfilled (e.g. clean clothes or a cut lawn) with less environmental impact and increased quality of life[45]. According to recent analyses by the business community, customers' long-term loyalty seems to be geared towards a service offered rather than to the provision of a product[46].

In some cases, purchasing services can be environmentally preferable compared to the purchase of corresponding products. Reduced environmental impacts have been documented for services like dining in a restaurant, providing floor-covering, employing a decorating firm, or using a laundry service, as opposed to eating at home, or buying carpeting, do-it-yourself equipment or a washing machine.

Policy challenges are:

- To reduce energy and material inputs relative to the service provided to the consumer, thereby minimizing negative environmental impacts resulting from production, distribution, use, and disposal;

- To extend the length of product life and to optimize product design for durability, repair, remanufacturing, and recycling;

- To encourage reuse, repair, remanufacturing, and recycling of products by promoting repair and exchange centers, or the sorting and composting of waste;

- To stimulate the production and consumption of environmentally preferable consumer goods, e.g. through the use of eco-labels;

- To encourage shifts from goods to services with clear environmental, social, and economic benefits; and

- To increase understanding about the factors that influence purchase and disposal of consumer goods, and about the role of media and advertising in shaping consumption patterns.

The most important information that policy makers concerned with more sustainable goods and services need is data and indicators on trends in sales of selected consumer goods and in shifts towards more sustainable behavior of consumers and producers, the average length of product life, and the role of marketing and advertising.

Possible indicators are:

Indicator	Comment
Retail sales of selected goods per capita (total expenditure or in physical terms)	• Monitors retail sales of electronics, home-appliances, and clothing. • Interesting areas for further research are more detailed studies on indicators of material throughput and the energy intensity of selected durable and non-durable consumer goods. • Depending on the product category, the indicator can be expressed in terms of total expenditure or in physical terms (volume). • Short term/medium term data-availability.

Average length of product life for major consumer durables (e.g. refrigerator, washing-machine, TV, car)	• Monitors durability of selected consumer goods. • More work is needed on this type of indicator. Product lifetime can be an ambiguous indicator, in part because new products can be better than older products from an environmental perspective (more efficient and cleaner). Also, the lifetime of a product can be influenced by fashion, which is hard to distinguish empirically from the "technical lifetime" of the product. • Attention should be given to the environmental effects of the product throughout its life-cycle. • Alternative indicators are: Actual product lifetime as compared to technical lifetime, Guarantee period of a product, and Frequency of model change.
Market share of more sustainably produced goods and services (%)	• Monitors social and environmental interest and awareness of consumers and producers. • Indicator needs further development. It might cover the following groups of goods and services: 1. Environmentally friendly (or preferable) products, including eco-labelled products; 2. Reused and recycled products; 3. Services replacing products while generating positive environmental effects.
Per capita paper consumption[47]	• Reflects potential for less paper-intensive communication. • Relates to water pollution and waste volume. • Might be supplemented by indicator of paper recycling. • Indicator reflects development.
Advertising indicator (to be determined)	• Indicator of role of media and advertising in shaping consumption and production patterns. • The role of advertising in influencing lifestyles, both in industrialized and in developing countries, requires more attention for assessing the impact of advertising in stimulating more or less sustainable consumption, and for analysing the opportunities that advertising gives as a tool in policy making.
Private final consumption expenditure (index and by product group)	• For measuring trends in private consumption levels. • Increasing/decreasing expenditure on certain product groups indicate changes in consumption patterns. • This indicator is of relevance for other consumption clusters as well.
Public final consumption (total)	• Indicator of the level of public consumption. • May be compared to total consumption (public and private).

2.6.3 Buildings and housekeeping

Housekeeping, i.e. the use and management of commercial and residential buildings, requires energy for heating, cooling, lighting, food storage and preparation, washing and other functions. It also involves a significant consumption of water and of construction materials. Choices with regard to the type of materials and the quantities of energy and water used can be made on the basis of cost-considerations, the availability of and information about alternatives, and incentives to use them. Similar choices and considerations intervene when a new building is constructed.

The outcomes of these choices and decisions can be measured by tracking trends in commercial and residential energy use, in the production and use of energy and water saving devices, and in the use of environmentally friendly materials.

Approximately 36 per cent of world primary energy is consumed by commercial and residential buildings, while levels of use are substantially higher in industrialized countries. In both residential and commercial buildings, the growth rate of energy use in developing countries (respectively 5.7 and 6.7 per cent per year) has surpassed that in industrialized countries (respectively 1.4 and 2.6 per cent per year) in recent years[48]. Energy use in residential buildings is about twice that of commercial buildings worldwide, though the energy demand in commercial buildings has grown more rapidly than demand in residential buildings for the past two decades[49].

In industrialized countries, population increase, decreasing household size, and an increased demand for various residential services such as air conditioning, appliances, and space and water heating have contributed to an increase in energy use in residential buildings.

In developing countries, higher incomes, urbanization and population growth, and the shift away from traditional fuels are major factors leading to higher demand for commercial energy in the residential sector[50]. Some of the above factors, in combination with an increase in the demand for services such as electric heating, computers, and other office equipment have contributed to growth in energy use in commercial buildings, both in industrialized and developing countries.

The technical potential for energy efficiency improvement in residential and commercial buildings is considerable (estimates for the United States range from 27 to 48%, for some European countries between 42 and 76%, and for some developing countries from 31 to 56 per cent)[51].

One way of enhancing energy-efficiency in residential and commercial buildings is the use of more efficient technologies and practices for buildings, including proper orientation, adequate insulation levels, high-quality windows, and building management and control systems[52]. In developing countries, ample room exists for efficiency improvements in connection with electricity use, e.g. for lighting and refrigeration. Examples from the noncommercial sector are the improvement of the efficiency of traditional appliances such as wood or kerosene stoves[53].

Energy consumption in residential and commercial buildings also depends on consumer behavior, including, thermostat settings, frequency of use of appliances and equipment, use of lighting, and use of windows and outside doors. Consumers can sometimes also decide to switch to alternative energy sources, such as solar photovoltaics, wind power, or ethanol fuel. The use of solar-cookers is an example from the alternative energy sector in developing countries. Consumer education as to ways to conserve energy and reduce energy bills can assist in reducing energy consumption.

The residential and commercial sectors are modest users of water, accounting for roughly 10% of current global consumption (see 2.5.3). In many OECD countries, the magnitude of household water use has remained stable since the end of the 1980s. However, demand is rising in some countries, in particular in countries experiencing rapid urbanization. In most cases, personal hygiene requires the highest amount of water. Important issues are an improved assessment of water use and water consumption needs, and better housekeeping involving the correction of inefficiencies in water delivery and use. Improvements in water using appliances can also contribute to water conservation.

The housing sector uses building materials and generates waste. Much progress can still be made in diminishing the use of environmentally unfriendly and unhealthy materials and products (e.g. paints, stains, and adhesives containing VOCs), and the generation of waste, for example through the use of more durable and long-lasting materials (e.g. ceramic floors), in order to minimize future replacement.

Measures aimed at increased use of collective facilities (e.g. collective laundries) can also contribute to resource conservation. House-keeping measures for the avoidance of waste are also important.

Even though this section has mainly focused on resource consumption in residential and commercial buildings, the choices households and commercial entities face prior to occupying a building are also of interest to policy makers.

For example, households and companies need to select an appropriate location. The location of a building relative to transportation facilities and to energy distribution and communication grids can have an important effect on the types and amount of resources consumed. The extent to which shops, means of public transportation, schools, and other important facilities are accessible in turn determines a whole range of other choices, including those related to mobility. The increased integration of environment and sustainability in spatial planning and decision making provides many opportunities for policy makers in developing more sustainable housing.

Decisions are also taken with respect to purchasing or renting an existing house or building or constructing a new one. Financial and other considerations play a role here. Control over architecture, design, and decoration increases when the decision to construct a new building is made. Considering the life-span of a house, decisions made at the drawing board on design and material use have large impacts on the degree of sustainability of housing facilities.

Policy challenges are:

- To increase understanding of the motivations underlying housing and house-keeping choices;
- To enhance the efficiency of energy and water use in housing by using more efficient technologies and practices for buildings, by improving housekeeping, and by increasing, where possible, the use of renewable energy sources;
- To integrate environmental considerations in architecture and the design of homes and appliances; and
- To increase the use of low-emission, less toxic and durable materials and products, and to minimize waste by using recyclable materials.

Key indicators are:

Indicator	Comment
Residential energy and water use per household (toe and liters)	• Monitors total water and energy use in households due to consumer behavior, housing equipment, and housing design and construction. • Closely linked to indicators for intensity of water use (See section on Water - 2.5.3) and energy consumption (See section on Energy - 2.5.1). • Chapter 18 of the WPISD includes the indicator Domestic consumption of water per capita. • In developing countries, particularly in rural areas, where there is inadequate access to clean water and commercial energy, it may be desirable to increase residential water and commercial energy consumption. • Data should be available in the short term.
Average household size (number of persons)	• Monitors the number of persons per household. • Data should be available in the short/medium term.
Use of recycled materials in construction (%)	• Monitors trends in more sustainable construction. • Close links exist with sections 2.5.2 (Materials) and 2.6.2 (Consumer goods and services).

2.6.4 Food

Apart from the fact that food fulfils basic nutritional needs, the consumption of food is intertwined with cultural habits and values, and culinary tastes and preferences. The choice of where one eats, for example at home or in a restaurant, is determined by similar motivations, together with time-availability for unpaid work and financial considerations. If the consumer prepares food at home, preparation-time, taste, availability, food price and quality, household-size, and health become important factors for selecting food-products.

Food consumption patterns contribute to environmental problems through energy and chemical use, intensified land use, and waste generated in the food production processing industry.

Food consumption patterns such as high consumption of meat and dairy products, elaborately packaged products, intensively grown produce, or frozen foods have environmental consequences, and may contribute to problems such as acidification, water pollution, climate change, and waste generation. Moreover, as was already mentioned in section 2.6.1, transport of food products over long distances can have significant environmental impacts.

Dietary preferences tend to change with increasing income in favor of meat and dairy products, which require much more land than grains and vegetables. Land in developing countries is now increasingly being used for growing grain feed, fodder and forage for livestock in order to export meat to industrialized countries.

Most consumers in industrialized countries can now enjoy a wide variety of food from all over the world at all times of the year, and the demand for semi- or fully prepared meals has risen[54]. Food processing can contribute to environmental problems. For example, energy use for fish processing increases when the fish is frozen. Frozen food generally has a high energy requirement for freezing and for keeping frozen until it is consumed.

An increasing number of consumers are interested in food produced with more environmentally friendly agricultural practices allowing for a reduced use of chemical fertilizers and pesticides (e.g. integrated pest management). Though it may not be possible to extend the area used for organic agriculture and other more environmentally sustainable practices substantially, the potential for extending such practices could be assessed. Developing countries can benefit from shifts towards an increased demand for organic agriculture by increasing their exports of organic agricultural commodities such as coffee and fruit[55].

Policy challenges are:

- To increase understanding of the underlying reasons for trends in food consumption;
- To shift demand toward more resource-efficient foods;
- To encourage the consumption of food grown with a minimum of environmentally harmful fertilizers or pesticides;
- To stimulate the market for more sustainably produced foods, in particular from developing countries; and
- To minimize waste generation resulting from food consumption.

Key indicators are:

Indicator	Comment
Daily caloric supply per capita (Calories/capita/day)	• Monitors the average caloric intake per capita. • Indicator can be specified for specific groups in the society with different per capita incomes. • The WPISD includes two indicators for chapter 6 (promoting human health), that are of relevance for food consumption: Proportion of potentially hazardous chemicals monitored in food, and Nutritional status of children.
Market share of more sustainably produced food (%)	• Monitors social and environmental interest and awareness of consumers and producers. • Alternative indicators suggested during the Workshop on indicators for chapter 4 were: Share of resource intensive food production, and Share of food from resource intensive production. • Indicator needs further development. The indicator might follow a sliding scale of more sustainably produced food, and might be measured through labels and product information. It should be a rough estimate of market share without requiring agreement on a precise definition of sustainably produced food. It can therefore include organically produced food and food produced with more environmental, social, and economic benefits than its shelf counterparts. • The WPISD includes two indicators for chapter 14 (promoting sustainable agriculture and rural development): Use of agricultural pesticides, and Use of fertilizers.

2.6.5 Recreation

Leisure and recreation involve different types of activities, including travel, staying in hotels and resorts, skiing, sailing, fishing, reading, watching TV, camping, and motor touring. The trends in the types of activities undertaken depend on factors such as available income, time, cultural background, and personal preferences.

The determining factors driving consumer choice and behavior in leisure activities are rarely included in policy analyses. In order to measure trends and track effectiveness of policy implementation, data on what portion of the day is taken up by work, un-paid work, and leisure is important.

In addition, the percentage of disposable income spent on leisure goods and services also gives policy makers a reading of the perceived need for leisure, and the importance attached to leisure as part of a consumer's day.

Leisure activities have differing degrees of environmental impacts. These impacts can either be caused directly by the activity itself (e.g. jet-skiing, hiking, golf, skiing), or more indirectly by the need for travel to remote destinations.

Certain types of recreation activities have a potentially positive effect on the environment, and tend to improve the broader social and economic aspects of sustainable development. Eco-tourism, hiking, and wildlife safaris, for example, have increased the demand for nature conservation and enhanced environmental planning and management, often providing income for local populations. The largest and most serious negative environmental impacts are due to growth in air and car travel to holiday destinations, and the growth in mass tourism causing water pollution and land degradation, particularly in coastal zones.

Some trends in developed countries indicate that an increased per capita disposable income combined with limited time available for leisure can lead to farther and faster travel to leisure destinations.

Travel and tourism has become the world's largest industry, accounting for over 10 percent of world economic activity and providing direct or indirect employment to over 250 million people. It is one of the fastest growing economic sectors, with international tourist arrivals growing by 5 per cent each year. In 1996, the World Tourism Organization estimated that international arrivals worldwide reached almost 600 million. It is estimated that this figure will increase by over 50% by 2010[56].

At present, 15 of the top 20 countries in terms of tourist revenues are developed countries (representing 60 per cent of the total market). The five leading tourism destinations in developing countries in terms of numbers of international arrivals are the Caribbean, China, Malaysia, Mexico, and Turkey, with about 11 per cent of the income share[57].

Two broad types of tourism can be distinguished: mass tourism, which makes up the bulk of today's industry and is characterized by package arrangements, and alternative tourism, including trekking, hiking, diving, and bird and animal watching.

Though alternative tourism is growing at 5 to 10 percent per year, the World Tourism Organization estimates that the maximum share of alternative tourism achievable is 10 percent[58]. Even though alternative tourism activities, and in particular the sub-set "eco-tourism", are generally less harmful for the environment than mass tourism, the goal of sustainable tourism applies to both categories.

Eco-tourism may not only be more sustainable than mass tourism, but can also provide revenues for maintaining areas of particular environmental importance. Carefully managed tourism to habitats with unusual wild animals or plants or other special characteristics can be crucial to providing the financial resources for preserving those habitats.

Policy challenges are:

- To understand the factors and motivations determining the time and money spent on various leisure activities;
- To minimize resource degradation and pollution from leisure and recreation activities by improving resource management and spatial planning, and providing adequate facilities and consumer information;
- To encourage recreation activities that are less harmful for the environment; and
- To develop eco-tourism and nature-based tourism, which can provide financial support for local populations and the conservation of natural resources and biodiversity.

As in the case of the transport sector, it should be noted that Agenda 21 has no separate chapter on tourism and/or recreation. Therefore, the WPISD only includes one indicator that could be related to the effects of recreation on the environment, i.e. Protected area as percent of total area (chapter 15, conservation of biological diversity). Tourism is, however, one of the 15 programme areas of the Programme of Action for the Sustainable Development of Small Island Developing States.

Policy making on this issue needs additional analysis and should address in particular aspects of resource intensity for selected recreation activities. Currently, it seems most important for policy making to have information on time and spending on recreational and other activities. This information would help to determine where to apply measures most effectively.

Important indicators are:

Indicator	Comment
Contribution of tourism/recreation to the economy (revenues from tourism/recreation as percentage of GDP)	• Indicator for the dependence of the economy on revenues from tourism/recreation, and possibly of the vulnerability of both the economy and the environment to fluctuations in tourism/recreation activities.

Time spent on leisure, paid and unpaid work, and traveling (hours per capita per day)	• Monitors time-allocation and distribution, and reflects lifestyles. • See also 2.6.1 (Mobility). • The policy application of this indicator needs further development. Interesting areas for research are the relationship between time spent on particular activities and lifestyles, consumer satisfaction, as well as the distribution of work. • Short term/medium term data-availability.
Spending on recreation as percentage of disposable income (%)	• Monitors the demand for recreation activities. • Short term/medium term data-availability.
Land used for recreation purposes as share of total land area	• Is included in the land use indicator (2.5.4).
Site stress indicator/index	• The indicator or index could include, for selected important recreation and tourism sites, indicators of site stress (e.g. Number of visitors per year/peak month), use intensity (e.g. Persons per hectare, Type of activity, Frequency of activity). • The World Tourism Organization is currently developing such an Index.
Share of alternative tourism over total tourism (%)	• Monitors trends in demand for alternative tourism. • Social and economic aspects of tourism should not be overlooked.

3 INDICATORS FOR MEASURING CHANGES IN CONSUMPTION AND PRODUCTION PATTERNS

3.1 Approaches to indicator classification and use

The most commonly used framework for developing environmental indicators, the Pressure-State-Response (PSR) framework, was developed by the OECD in the early 1990's. In reaction to an increasing interest in the measurement of environmental damage and in evaluating the effectiveness of environmental policy measures, the OECD Council approved a Recommendation on Environmental Indicators and Information, instructing the OECD Environment Policy Committee to *(...) "further develop core sets of reliable, readable, measurable and policy-relevant environmental indicators" (...).* In 1993, the OECD Group on the State of the Environment conducted a series of Workshops, developed a common conceptual framework, and defined a core set of indicators, using the Pressure-State-Response (PSR) framework.

The PSR framework is based on the idea that human activities exert pressure on the environment (represented by pressure indicators), thereby changing the quality of the environment and the quantity of natural resources (represented by state indicators). Society responds to these changes through environmental, economic and sectoral policies (represented by response indicators). Policy responses affect individual and collective actions (I) to mitigate, adapt to or prevent human-induced negative impacts on the environment, (ii) to halt or reverse environmental damage already inflicted, and (iii) to preserve and conserve natural resources[59].

In establishing the Work Programme on Indicators of Sustainable Development (WPISD), the Commission on Sustainable Development has adopted the PSR framework developed by the OECD, while going beyond environmental aspects, and identifying three further dimensions of sustainable development, namely social, economic, and institutional aspects.

In this expanded version of the framework, called the "Driving Force-State-Response" (DSR) framework, the concept of pressure has been replaced by that of "driving forces", in order to accommodate the inclusion of social, economic, and institutional aspects of sustainable development. The term "driving force" indicates an impact on sustainable development, which can either be positive or negative. Indicators in the "state" category gives an indication of the state of sustainable development, and response indicators indicate societal responses to changes in sustainable development.

Other frameworks have been developed and used, for example, by the United Nations Statistical Division, UNEP and the European Environment Agency. However, these frameworks are very similar to the PSR and the DSR frameworks, and indicators developed and used in these and other contexts could easily be placed within the DSR framework.

The recently initiated work on "Sustainable Consumption Indicators" of the OECD is structured around the following major themes deriving from the PSR framework: environmentally significant consumption trends and patterns; interaction between consumption trends and patterns and the environment and natural resources; and economic and policy aspects. This is very much in line with the DSR framework and the key resources and consumption clusters outlined in this paper. The DSR framework allows for the presentation of all aspects of sustainable development, and it is simple and easy to understand and use. Furthermore, the use of the DSR framework facilitates incorporation into the set of indicators of sustainable development of the WPISD, and is in line with frameworks used by other organizations and governments.

Research, development and experience in the scientific community, governments and organizations may result in the development of more advanced analytical frameworks that more accurately reflect the complex dynamics of changing consumption and production patterns. In the longer term, the use of such frameworks should be carefully reviewed.

3.2 A core set of indicators for changing consumption and production patterns

3.2.1 Selection of a core set of indicators

Two sets of indicator selection criteria were used for the selection of the provisional core set of indicators. A first set of criteria is based on key considerations from the consumption-production perspective, and the second set comprises criteria used for the selection of indicators for the CSD Work Programme on Indicators of Sustainable Development. Both sets are outlined in Box 9.

With regard to the second set of selection criteria, it should be noted that it is not yet feasible, at this stage, to fully comply with the "Bellagio principles"[60], or to provide information on the data availability and quality.

Box 9 Consumption-Production Selection Criteria

The core-set of indicators for measuring changes in consumption and production patterns should:

- Include all key resources and consumption clusters (representing various types of end-use) that are susceptible to policy intervention and relate to critical environmental trends;
- Reflect both total consumption and use intensity;
- Include indicators that simultaneously cover various key resources and consumption clusters, while also allowing for (crosscutting) indicators that do not fit into any of these categories;
- Reflect chapter 4, and in particular the "added value" of the production-consumption approach;
- Reflect concepts which are widely used in sustainable development policy analysis (e.g. eco-efficiency);
- Include indicators for monitoring progress towards short term and long term targets and objectives (e.g. quantified targets for emission reduction, and targets for resource productivity - e.g. Factor 4 or 10);
- Take into account the institutional capacities and programmes of major institutions and actors; and,
- Be consistent with and complementary to a possible wider framework of indicators and indices.

Box 9 (continued)

Indicator Selection Criteria

The indicators selected for the core set should be:

- Primarily national in scale or scope (countries may also wish to use the indicators at state or provincial levels);
- Relevant to the main objective of assessing progress towards sustainable development;
- Understandable, i.e. simple, clear and unambiguous;
- Realizable within the capacities of national governments, given their logistic, time, technical and other constraints;
- Conceptually well founded;
- Limited in number, remaining open-ended and adaptable to future developments;
- Broad in coverage of Agenda 21, and all aspects of sustainable development (in this context, focused on the key issues of chapter 4 of agenda 21);
- Representative of international consensus, to the extent possible; and
- Dependent on data that are readily available or available at a reasonable cost-benefit ratio, adequately documented, of known quality and updated at regular intervals.

3.2.2 The provisional core set of indicators for changing consumption and production patterns

This section introduces the provisional core set of indicators for changing consumption and production patterns. Following the arguments in section 3.1, The Driving Force-State-Response framework is used for categorizing and presenting the core set of indicators. It should be noted that the social-economic-environmental-institutional classification used in the context of the CSD Work Programme on Indicators of Sustainable Development (WPISD) is not reflected here. According to the WPISD, indicators for chapter 4 of Agenda 21 are all categorized in the economic category. The indicators proposed here are all relevant to the economic category, but many are also relevant to the environmental, social and institutional categories.

The core set does not include all the indicators selected for chapter 4 under the WPISD framework, and has a minimum of overlap with indicators selected for other chapters of Agenda 21. Attention has also been paid towards establishing, to the extent possible, a balance among Driving force, State, and Response indicators.

As in the WPISD framework, the core set is intended to allow governments to choose which indicators to use at the national level. Therefore, the consumption-production related environmental concerns reflected by the indicators do not necessarily need to be of equal importance in each county. The selection of core indicators focuses on those key resources and consumption clusters that have significant environmental impacts and seem particularly susceptible to public policy intervention.

The core set of indicators for changing consumption and production patterns will be an input to the WPISD and the revision of its indicators for sustainable development in 1999-2000. In the near future, the definitions and methodological descriptions of the core set indicators for chapter 4 will be described and summarized in the form of methodology sheets (see ANNEX 1). In addition, national Governments may embark, in cooperation with international organizations, on a first round of testing of the core set or parts of the core set.

The indicators selected for the core set should be of relevance for industrialized and developing countries, and for countries with economies in transition. The core set of indicators has a particular relevance for policy makers in developed countries, since these countries are to take the lead in making consumption and production patterns more sustainable (Agenda 21, chapter 4).

The indicators may help policy makers in industrialized countries choose appropriate policy measures aimed at eco-efficiency improvements and the achievement of more sustainable consumption practices and lifestyles. For developing countries and economies in transition, the indicators could be used to monitor the development of consumption and production patterns, while promoting the development process. The suggested indicators can in most cases be applied at a global, regional, national, and local scale, depending on the objective for which they are used.

Furthermore, the core set of indicators is provisional, and should evolve over time in a dynamic process, reflecting changes in priorities related to sustainable consumption and production patterns.

The provisional core set of indicators for changing consumption and production patterns is outlined in Table 1. Table 2 presents the same indicators in the Driving Force - State - Response Framework. Box 10 summarizes the areas for further research identified in the process.

Box 10 Some key areas for further work

For energy, additional work is needed to define the most appropriate combination of indicators to monitor trends in affordability of energy, i.e. the extent to which energy becomes cheaper or more expensive over time. Indicators for energy prices could be related to indicators for disposable income. Affordability of energy could be calculated for different income groups and uses. If appropriate, use could be made of elasticity indicators of energy demand.

Some areas related to mobility and transport need more attention. It would be interesting, for example, to draw on national experience for selecting a group of key indicators for the sector, particularly because this work has not yet been undertaken in the context of Agenda 21 and the WPISD. Indicators for trends in mobility and transport related to the "electronic age" and "information super highway" (e.g. telecommuting, teleshopping) merit attention in the near future.

In the area of consumer goods and services, indicators for the length of product life (both from a technical and fashion standpoint), and indicators for more sustainably produced products and services need to be defined further. More efforts could also be undertaken to identify policy-relevant indicators for the role of media and advertising on consumption and production patterns.

Some additional indicators could also be developed for recreation and tourism, in particular for monitoring trends in consumption patterns and in the way individuals spend their time.

Finally, more work on indicators reflecting social and human development aspects of production patterns is needed.

Since only some of the work suggested in Box 10 will be carried out by the CSD Secretariat, other actors are invited to explore these issues further, in order to contribute to a continuous improvement of the current provisional core set of indicators for changing consumption and production patterns.

Table 1 Core Set of Indicators for Changing Consumption and Production Patterns

KEY RESOURCES		
ENERGY		
1.	Annual energy consumption per capita	Monitors energy consumption.
2.	Intensity of energy use	Monitors energy use per unit of production/service (for selected sectors).
3.	Share of renewable energy in total energy consumption	Monitors the development of renewable energy sources.
4.	Energy prices	Monitors energy prices in relation to GDP and disposable income.
MATERIALS		
5.	Total material requirement	Monitors total material throughput, including hidden or indirect material flows required for a national economy.
6.	Intensity of material use	Monitors material use per unit of production/service (for selected sectors).
WATER		
7.	Intensity of water use	Monitors water use per unit of production/service for selected sectors.
LAND		
8.	Land use	Monitors land use (forestry, agriculture, settlements, infrastructure, and recreation).
CONSUMPTION CLUSTERS		
MOBILITY		
9.	Distance travelled per capita by mode of transport	Monitors the use of different modes of transport (foot, bicycle, train, boat, car, bus, plane).
10.	Number of road vehicles	Monitors the total number of vehicles (possibly by type and fuel efficiency).
CONSUMER GOODS AND SERVICES		
11.	Retail sales of selected goods per capita	Monitors retail sales of goods (e.g. electronics, home-appliances, clothing).
12.	Market share of more sustainably produced goods and services	Monitors social and environmental interest of consumers and producers.
BUILDINGS AND HOUSEKEEPING		
13	Residential energy and water use per household	Monitors total water and energy use in households due to consumer behaviour and housing design and construction.
14.	Average household size	Monitors the number of persons per household.
FOOD		
15.	Market share of more sustainably produced food	Monitors social and environmental interest of consumers and producers.
RECREATION		
16	Spending on recreation as share of disposable income	Monitors the demand for recreation activities.
17.	Time spent on leisure, paid and unpaid work, and travelling	Monitors time-allocation and distribution, and reflects lifestyles.

Table 2 Core Set Indicators in the Driving Force - State - Response framework

ISSUE CHAPTER 4 OF AGENDA 21	DRIVING FORCE INDICATORS	STATE INDICATORS	RESPONSE INDICATORS
CATEGORY: KEY RESOURCES			
Energy	-Annual energy consumption per capita	-Intensity of energy use -Share of renewable energy in total energy consumption	-Energy prices
Materials	-Total material requirement (TMR)	-Intensity of material use	
Water	-Intensity of water use		
Land		-Land use	
CATEGORY: CONSUMPTION CLUSTERS			
Mobility	- Distance travelled per capita by mode of transport - Number of road vehicles		
Consumer goods and services	-Retail sales of selected goods per capita		-Market share of more sustainably produced goods and services
Buildings and housekeeping	-Residential energy and water use per household	-Average household size	
Food			-Market share of more sustainably produced food
Recreation	-Spending on recreation as share of disposable income -Time spent on leisure, paid and unpaid work, and travelling		

REFERENCES

- Adriaanse, "Environmental Policy Performance Indicators - a Study on the Development of Indicators for Environmental Policy in the Netherlands", 1993.

- ANPED, The Northern Alliance for Sustainability, Priorities and Issues, 1997.

- de Boer, Margaretha, "The Environment, Space and Living Quality - Time for Sustainability", The Hague, 1995.

- State Statistical Bureau, People's Republic of China, China Statistical Yearbook 1995.

- Commission on Sustainable Development, Fourth session, (18 April - 3 May 1996), "Changing Consumption and Production Patterns", Report of the Secretary-General, E/CN.17/1996/5, and Addendum, E/CN.17/1996/5/Add.1.

- Commission on Sustainable Development, Report on the Fourth Session (18 April - 3 May 1996), Economic and Social Council, Official Records, 1996, Supplement 8.

- European Commission, Eurostat, "Indicators of Sustainable Development - A Pilot Study following the Methodology of the United Nations Commission of Sustainable Development", 1997.

- European Forest Institute and Norwegian Forest Research Institute, "Long-term Trends and Prospects in World Supply and Demand for Wood and Implications for Sustainable Forest Management: A Synthesis", July 1996.

- Factor 10 Club, "Statement to Government and Business Leaders - A ten-fold leap in energy and resource efficiency", 1997.

- Friends of the Earth International, "Ten times better: Fair Shares in Environmental Space", Brochure, 1997.

- Friends of the Earth Netherlands, "Sustainable Consumption - A Global Perspective", 1996.

- Fussler, Claude and James, Peter, "Driving Eco-Innovation - a breakthrough discipline for innovation and sustainability", 1996.

- International Institute for Environment and Development, "Unlocking Trade Opportunities - Case Studies of Export Success from Developing Countries", 1997.

- International Institute for Sustainable Development (IISD), "Trade and Sustainable Development - A Survey of the Issues and A New Research Agenda", 1992.

- Ministry of Environment, Norway, "Report of the Symposium on Sustainable Consumption", 19-20 January 1994, Oslo, Norway.

- Ministry of Environment, Norway, "Report of the Oslo Ministerial Round Table - Conference on Sustainable Production and Consumption", 6-10 February 1995.

- Ministry of Housing, Physical Planning, and the Environment, Netherlands, "Social Instruments to Influence Consumption", August 1995.

- Ministry of Housing, Physical Planning, and the Environment and Ministry of Economic Affairs, Netherlands, "Sustainable Industrial Development - Sharing Responsibilities in a Competitive World - Chairman's report of the Conference", April 1996.

- Ministry of Housing, Physical Planning, and the Environment, Netherlands, "The Best of Both Worlds - Sustainability and Quality Lifestyles in the 21th Century", 1993.

- Moldan, B., Billharz, S., and Matravers, R., "Scope 58 - Sustainability Indicators: A Report on the Project on Indicators of Sustainable Development", 1997.

- NCDO (Nationale Commissie voor Internationale Samenwerking en Duurzame Ontwikkeling), "Creatieve Democratie - Kroniek van Duurzaam Nederland", 1996.

- Nordman, Bruce, "Celebrating consumption", 1995 (contribution consultative round).

- OECD, "Economic Instruments for Environmental Management in Developing Countries", Paris, 1993.

- OECD, "Environmental Indicators, OECD Core Set", Paris, 1994.

- OECD, "Indicators for the integration of environmental concerns into energy policies", Environment Monographs no 79, Paris, 1993.

- OECD, "Indicators for the integration of environmental concerns into transport policies", Environment Monographs no 79, Paris, 1993.

- OECD, "OECD Workshop on Sustainable Consumption and Production: Clarifying the Concepts", Rosendal, Norway, 2-4 July 1995, Final Report.

- OECD, "OECD Environmental data - Compendium 1997", Paris, 1997.

- OECD, "Sustainable Consumption and Production", Paris, 1997.

- RIVM, "Modeling Global Biochemical Cycles - an integrated assessment approach", Global Dynamics and Sustainable Development Programme, GLOBO Report Series, No 4, 1994.

- RIVM, "Modeling Global Biochemical Cycles - an integrated assessment approach", Global Dynamics and Sustainable Development Programme, GLOBO Report Series, No 7, 1995.

- Spangenberg J.H. and Schmidt-Bleek, F, "Concepts for Sustainability", Wuppertal Institute for Climate, Environment, Energy Division for Material Flows and Structural Change, 1996.

- Rees W. and Wackernagel M., "Ecological Footprints and Appropriated Carrying Capacity: Measuring the Natural Capital Requirements of the Human Economy", in "Investing in Natural Capital: the Ecological Economics Approach to Sustainability", A.M Jansson, M. Hammer, C. Folke, and R. Constanza, eds. Washington Island Press, 1994.

- Republic of Korea, "Report of the Workshop on Policy Measures for Changing Consumption Patterns", (30 August - 1 September 1995, Seoul, Korea).

- Stockholm Environment Institute, Chapter 9 "Industrial Metabolism - closing the materials cycle", 1993, in: "Clean Production Strategies - Developing Preventive Environmental Management in the Industrial Economy", edited by Tim Jackson, R.U. Ayres.

- The Delphi Group, "Financing Sustainable Consumption and Production: Engaging Capital Markets", April 1997.

- The Economist - A survey of Travel and Tourism, January 1998.

- Environment Agency, Government of Japan, "Report of Expert Workshop on Methodologies for Indicators of Sustainable Development", Glen Cove, Long Island, New York (5-8 February 1996).

- Tietenberg, T. "Market-based Mechanisms for Controlling Pollution: Lessons from the US", Chapter 2 in: Sterner, T. "Economic Policies for Sustainable Development, Economy and Environment, Volume 7, 1994.

- TNO, CBS, and the University of Utrecht, "Trendanalyse Consumptie en Milieu", Ministry of Housing, Physical Planning, and the Environment, Netherlands, 1996.

- United Nations Centre for Human Settlements (Habitat), "Changing Consumption Patterns - Report of an Expert Group Meeting", New York, 1997.

- United Nations Conference on Trade and Development (UNCTAD), "Environment, international competitiveness and development: lessons from empirical studies - The policy debate on trade, environment, and development", (TD/B/WG.6/10), 1995.

- United Nations Conference on Trade and Development (UNCTAD), "Identification of means through which competitiveness of natural products with environmental advantages could be improved - Reducing environmental stress of consumption without affecting consumer satisfaction", TD/B/CN.1/25, 1994.

- United Nations Conference on Trade and Development (UNCTAD), "Examination of the manner in which prices of natural commodities and their synthetic competitors could reflect environmental costs, taking into account policies relating to the use and management of natural resources and sustainable development", (TD/B/CN.1/29), 1995.

- United Nations Conference on Trade and Development (UNCTAD), "Newly emerging environmental policies with a possible trade impact: a preliminary discussion", (TD/B/WG.6/9), 1995.

- United Nations, "Agenda 21: the United Nations Programme of Action from Rio", 1992.

- United Nations, Department for Policy Coordination and Sustainable Development, "Measuring Changes in Consumption and Production Patterns", New York, 1996.

- United Nations, Department for Policy Coordination and Sustainable Development, "Indicators of Sustainable Development: Methodology Sheets, Background Paper 15", prepared for the Commission on Sustainable Development, Fourth Session, 18 April - 3 May 1996.

- United Nations, Department for Policy Coordination and Sustainable Development, "Indicators of Sustainable Development: Indicators of Sustainable Development Framework and Methodologies", August 1996.

- United Nations Department for Policy Coordination and Sustainable Development, Division for Sustainable Development, "Critical Trends - Global Change and Sustainable Development", New York, 1997.

- United Nations Department for Policy Coordination and Sustainable Development, Division for Sustainable Development, "Potentials and Policy Implications of Energy and Material Efficiency Improvement", 1997.

- United Nations, General Assembly, Nineteenth special session, Overall Review and Appraisal of the Implementation of Agenda 21, A/S-19/29, 27 June 1997.

- United Nations, "Work programme on Indicators of Sustainable Development of the Commission on Sustainable Development", February 1996, Division for Sustainable Development, United Nations Department for Policy Coordination and Sustainable Development.

- United Nations, "Work programme of Indicators of Sustainable Development of the Commission on Sustainable Development", September 1996, Division for Sustainable Development, United Nations Department for Policy Coordination and Sustainable Development.

- University of Maastricht, Catholic University of Brabant, for the Ministry of Housing, Physical Planning, and the Environment, Netherlands, "Tijd in relatie tot duurzaam consumeren", 1997.

- Wackernagel, "How big is our ecological footprint? Using the concept of Appropriated Carrying Capacity for Measuring Sustainability", University of British Columbia, 1993.

- Weizsäcker, von, E., Lovins, A.B., Lovins, L.H. "Factor Four - Doubling Wealth, Halving Resource Use", 1997.

- World Business Council for Sustainable Development, Summary of "A Changing Future for Paper", An independent study on the sustainability of the pulp and paper industry', prepared for the WBCSD by the International Institute for Environment and Development, 1996.

- World Meteorological Organization and Stockholm Environment Institute, "Comprehensive Assessment of the Freshwater Resources of the World", New York, 1997.

- World Resources Institute, World Resources 1994 - 1995 - A guide to the Global Environment. People and the Environment. Resource Consumption - Population Growth - Women, 1994.

- World Resources Institute, United Nations Environment Programme, United Nations Development Programme, The World Bank, "World Resources - a Guide to the Global Environment", 1996-1997.

- World Resources Institute, Wuppertal Institute, Netherlands Ministry of Housing, Spatial Planning, and Environment, National Institute for Environmental Studies, "Resource Flows: the Material Basis of Industrial Economies ", 1997.

- World Tourism Organization, "What tourism managers need to know - A practical guide to the Development and Use of Indicators of Sustainable Tourism", 1995

- Worldwatch Institute, Brown, L., Renner, M., Flavin, C., "Vital Signs 1997 - The Environmental Trends that are Shaping our Future", 1997.

- Wuppertal Institute, "Towards Sustainable Europe", January 1995.

ANNEXES

ANNEX 1	Sample methodology sheet
ANNEX 2	Some issues linked to changing consumption and production patterns
ANNEX 3	CSD Working List of indicators of Sustainable Development
ANNEX 4	List of participants of the consultative round and the Workshop

ANNEX 1

Sample Methodology Sheet

(from "Indicators of Sustainable Development: Framework and Methodologies")

ANNUAL ENERGY CONSUMPTION		
Economic	**Chapter 4**	**Driving Force**

1. Indicator

(a) **Name:** Annual energy consumption per capita.
(b) **Brief Definition**: The amount of energy - liquid, solid, gaseous or electricity - used by an individual in a given year in a given geographical area.
(c) **Unit of Measurement**: Gigajoules.

2. **Placement in Framework**

(a) **Agenda 21:** Chapter 4: Changing Consumption Patterns.
(b) **Type of Indicator**: Driving Force.

3. **Significance (Policy Relevance)**

(a) **Purpose:** The purpose of this indicator is to measure energy consumption.

(b) **Relevance to Sustainable/Unsustainable Development**: Energy use is a key aspect of consumption and production. Traditionally energy has been regarded as the engine of economic progress. However, its production, use, and byproducts have resulted in major impacts on the environment. The decoupling of energy use from development represents a major challenge of sustainable development. The long term aim is for development and prosperity to continue through gains in energy efficiency rather than increased production.

(c) **Linkages to Other Indicators:** This indicator is closely linked with many other economic and environmental indicators, such as population growth, transport fuel consumption, environmentally adjusted domestic product, proven energy reserves, consumption of renewable to non-renewable energy resources, land use change, energy use in agriculture, emissions of greenhouse gases, production of ozone depleting substances, generation of waste, etc.

(d) **Targets:** Not available.

(e) **International Conventions and Agreements:** Not available.

4. Methodological Description and Underlying Definitions

(a) **Underlying Definitions and Concepts:** The elements comprising this indicator are production, population and consumption data. The data on production refer to the first stage of production. For example, for hard coal the data refer to mine production; for crude petroleum and natural gas, to production at oil and gas wells and processing plants; for electricity to the gross production of generating plants. The data on consumption refer to "apparent consumption" and are derived from the formula which takes into account production, imports, exports, and stock changes.

(b) **Measurement Methods:** This indicator is computed by calculating the ratio of consumption of energy in a specific area/country/region to the population in that area/country/region.

(c) **The Indicator in the DSR Framework:** This indicator represents a major Driving Force within the economy.

(d) **Limitations of the Indicator:** Since this indicator is calculated by the aggregation of different consumption data within an area/country/region it may not accurately measure variations in the rates of consumption within that area/country/region. This can lead to invalid calculations and interpretations, and mis-allocation of resources.

The indicator is not as sensitive a measure of energy intensity and efficiency as some others, for example environmentally adjusted domestic product.

(e) **Alternative Indicator Definitions:** Disaggregation of the indicator into sectoral components such as agriculture or manufacturing, would permit assessment of energy requirements per unit of output. On the other hand, total energy consumption, provides a more direct measure of production patterns and the implications for the environment, while energy consumption as per unit of Gross Domestic Product provides a better reflection of energy efficiency.

5. Assessment of the Availability of Data from National and International Sources

Energy commodity data for production and consumption, and population data are regularly available for most countries at the national level; and for some countries, at the sub-national level. Both types of data are compiled by and available from national statistical offices and country publications.

6. Agencies Involved in Development of Indicator

(a) **Lead Agency:** The lead agency is the United Nations Statistical Division, department of Economics and Social Information and Policy Analysis (DESIPA). The contact point is the Director, Statistics Division, DESIPA; fax no. (1 212) 963 9851.

(b) **Other Organizations:** Other organizations involved in the indicator development include: national statistical offices, the International Energy Agency, the Organisation for Economic Co-operation and Development (OECD), and Eurostat.

7. Further Information

United Nations. *Energy Statistics Yearbook.*

ANNEX 2 Some issues linked to changing consumption and production patterns

Trade and the Environment

The trade-environment "debate" can be subdivided into 2 categories: (a) the impact of trade on the environment, and (b) the impact of environmental protection measures on trade. In relation to changing consumption and production patterns, there may be possible conflicts between trade policies and policies aimed at changing current consumption and production patterns - and the consequences thereof for developing countries (e.g. effects of policies such as eco-labeling initiatives, voluntary industry agreements, or policies aimed at dematerialization), and the possible advantages for developing countries of fair trade and trade in environmentally friendly products for Western consumer markets.

Technology

Technological factors are of particular importance in changing production patterns. Technology covers a large range of issues, including R&D, cleaner production processes, dematerialization of consumption, eco-efficiency and resource productivity improvements, and technology transfer to developing countries. Policies aimed at promoting these technological changes, and helping small enterprises cover the costs of adopting cleaner and more efficient technologies are receiving increasing attention.

Health

Causal links between consumption and production patterns in areas such as water use, agricultural land use, energy use, transportation and industrial practices, and their relation to outdoor and indoor air quality, water and soil quality, and food quality are subject of much research. However, more analyses are needed in order to determine the effects of consumption and production patterns and the resulting environmental changes on the frequency and severity of health problems such as hormone disruption, lung and cardiovascular diseases, tropical diseases, cancer, poisoning, and reproductive and immunological disorders. Health considerations are already an important driving force for changes in consumption patterns in a considerable number of countries (e.g. increasing interest in "organic" food), and could very well become an even more important consideration in the future.

Human Settlements

Metropolitan areas, cities, and towns tend to drive consumption and production patterns; not only because of the density of consumption-related activities taking place in cities (ranging from transportation, water and energy use, and waste generation), and because cities provide an important leverage point for achieving change, but also because cities are often characterized by a large population exerting pressure on a relatively small land-area.

Employment

Since unemployment is a major problem in many countries, the "jobs-versus-environment debate receives considerable attention. Some claim that changes in consumption and production patterns will lead to employment creation, since they will trigger investment in more efficient equipment and services, raising overall economic productivity. In addition, policies such as "ecological tax reform", support for technological innovation, and more environmentally friendly procurement policies would generate new jobs. Others, however, believe that the costs incurred by the changes would slow down overall economic growth and employment creation. These negative effects on employment would be reinforced by the "migration" of resource-inefficient enterprises to countries without eco-efficiency policies.

ANNEX 3

CSD Working List of Indicators of Sustainable Development (as of September 1996)

CHAPTERS OF AGENDA 21	DRIVING FORCE INDICATORS	STATE INDICATORS	RESPONSE INDICATORS
CATEGORY: SOCIAL			
Chapter 3: Combating poverty	-Unemployment rate	-Head count index of poverty -Poverty gap index -Squared poverty gap index -Gini index of income inequality -Ratio of average female wage to male wage	
Chapter 5: Demographic dynamics and sustainability	-Population growth rate -Net migration rate -Total fertility rate	-Population density	
Chapter 36: Promoting education, public awareness and training	-Rate of change of school-age population -Primary school enrolment ratio (gross and net) -Secondary school enrolment ratio (gross and net) -Adult literacy rate	-Children reaching grade 5 of primary education -School life expectancy -Difference between male and female school enrolment ratios -Women per hundred men in the labour force	-GDP spent on education
Chapter 6: Protecting and promoting human health		-Basic sanitation: Percent of population with adequate excreta disposal facilities -Access to safe drinking water -Life expectancy at birth -Adequate birth weight -Infant mortality rate -Maternal mortality rate -Nutritional status of children	-Immunization against infectious childhood diseases -Contraceptive prevalence -Proportion of potentially hazardous chemicals monitored in food -National health expenditure devoted to local health care -Total national health expenditure related to GNP
Chapter 7: Promoting sustainable human settlement development	-Rate of growth of urban population -Per capita consumption of fossil fuel by motor vehicle transport -Human and economic loss due to natural disasters	-Percent of population in urban areas -Area and population of urban formal and informal settlements -Floor area per person -House price to income ratio	-Infrastructure expenditure per capita

CHAPTERS OF AGENDA 21	DRIVING FORCE INDICATORS	STATE INDICATORS	RESPONSE INDICATORS
CATEGORY: ECONOMIC			
Chapter 2: International cooperation to accelerate sustainable development in countries and related domestic policies	-GDP per capita -Net investment share in GDP -Sum of exports and imports as a percent of GDP	-Environmentally adjusted Net Domestic Product -Share of manufactured goods in total merchandise exports	
Chapter 4: Changing consumption patterns	-Annual energy consumption -Share of natural-resource intensive industries in manufacturing value-added	-Proven mineral reserves -Proven fossil fuel energy reserves -Lifetime of proven energy reserves -Intensity of material use -Share of manufacturing value-added in GDP -Share of consumption of renewable energy resources	
Chapter 33: Financial resources and mechanisms	-Net resources transfer / GNP -Total ODA given or received as a percentage of GNP	-Debt / GNP -Debt service / export	-Environmental protection expenditures as a percent of GDP -Amount of new or additional funding for sustainable development
Chapter 34: Transfer of environmentally sound technology, cooperation and capacity-building	-Capital goods imports -Foreign direct investments	-Share of environmentally sound capital goods imports	-Technical cooperation grants
CATEGORY: ENVIRONMENTAL			
Chapter 18: Protection of the quality and supply of freshwater resources	-Annual withdrawals of ground and surface water -Domestic consumption of water per capita	-Groundwater reserves -Concentration of faecal coliform in freshwater -Biochemical oxygen demand in water bodies	-Waste-water treatment coverage -Density of hydrological networks
Chapter 17: Protection of the oceans, all kinds of seas and coastal areas	-Population growth in coastal areas -Discharges of oil into coastal waters -Releases of nitrogen and phosphorus to coastal waters	-Maximum sustained yield for fisheries -Algae index	

CHAPTERS OF AGENDA 21	DRIVING FORCE INDICATORS	STATE INDICATORS	RESPONSE INDICATORS
Chapter 10: Integrated approach to the planning and management of land resources	-Land use change	-Changes in land condition	-Decentralized local-level natural resource management
Chapter 12: Managing fragile ecosystems: combating desertification and drought	-Population living below poverty line in dryland areas	-National monthly rainfall index -Satellite derived vegetation index -Land affected by desertification	
Chapter 13: Managing fragile ecosystems: sustainable mountain development	-Population change in mountain areas	-Sustainable use of natural resources in mountain areas -Welfare of mountain populations	
Chapter 14: Promoting sustainable agriculture and rural development	-Use of agricultural pesticides -Use of fertilizers -Irrigation percent of arable land -Energy use in agriculture	-Arable land per capita -Area affected by salinization and waterlogging	-Agricultural education
Chapter 11: Combating deforestation	-Wood harvesting intensity	-Forest area change	-Managed forest area ratio -Protected forest area as a percent of total forest area
Chapter 15: Conservation of biological diversity		-Threatened species as a percent of total native species	-Protected area as a percent of total area
Chapter 16: Environmentally sound management of biotechnology			-R & D expenditure for biotechnology -Existence of national biosafety regulations or guidelines
Chapter 9: Protection of the atmosphere	-Emissions of greenhouse gasses -Emissions of sulphur oxides -Emissions on nitrogen oxides -Consumption of ozone depleting substances	-Ambient concentrations of pollutants in urban areas	-Expenditure on air pollution abatement
Chapter 21: Environmentally sound management of solid wastes and sewage-related issues	-Generation of industrial and municipal solid waste -Household waste disposed per capita		-Expenditure on waste management -Waste recycling and reuse -Municipal waste disposal

CHAPTERS OF AGENDA 21	DRIVING FORCE INDICATORS	STATE INDICATORS	RESPONSE INDICATORS
Chapter 19: Environmentally sound management of toxic chemicals		-Chemically induced acute poisonings	-Number of chemicals banned or severely restricted
Chapter 20: Environmentally sound management of hazardous wastes	-Generation of hazardous wastes -Imports and exports of hazardous wastes	-Area of land contaminated by hazardous wastes	-Expenditure on hazardous waste treatment
Chapter 22: Safe and environmentally sound management of radioactive wastes	-Generation of radioactive wastes		
CATEGORY: INSTITUTIONAL			
Chapter 8: Integrating environment and development in decision-making			-Sustainable development strategies -Programme of integrated environmental and economic accounting -Mandated Environmental Impact Assessment -National councils for sustainable development
Chapter 35: Science for sustainable development		-Potential scientists and engineers per million population	-Scientists and engineers engaged in R & D per million population -Expenditure on R & D as a percent of GDP
Chapter 37: National mechanisms and international cooperation for capacity-building in developing countries			
Chapter 38: International institutional arrangements			
Chapter 39: International legal instruments and mechanisms			-Ratification of global agreements -Implementation of ratified global agreements

CHAPTERS OF AGENDA 21	**DRIVING FORCE INDICATORS**	**STATE INDICATORS**	**RESPONSE INDICATORS**
Chapter 40: Information for decision-making		-Main telephone lines per 100 inhabitants -Access to information	-Programmes for national environmental statistics
Chapter 23-32: Strengthening the role of major groups			-Representation of major groups in national councils for sustainable development -Representatives of ethnic minorities and indigenous people in national councils for sustainable development -Contribution of NGOs to sustainable development

ANNEX 4

List of participants of the Consultative Round and the Workshop

Participants to the Consultative Round:

- Helene Bank, Norwegian NGO Forum for Environment and Development, Norway
- Manus van Brakel, Milieudefensie, Amsterdam, Netherlands
- Rae Kwon Chung, Permanent Mission of the Republic of Korea, New York, USA
- Robert Donkers, European Commission, Brussels, Belgium
- Jeremy Eppel, OECD, Paris, France
- Claude Fussler, Dow Europe, Horgen, Switzerland
- David Gershon, Global Action Plan, Woodstock, USA
- Yannick Glemarec, UNDP, Beijing, China
- Paul Hofseth, Ministry of Environment, Oslo, Norway
- R. Hull, European Commission, Brussels, Belgium
- Sitanon Jesdapipat, Thai Environment Institute, Bangkok, Thailand
- Pavel Kasyanov, Ministry of Environmental Protection and Natural Resources, Moscow, Russia
- Jaeyun Ko, Ministry of Environment, Seoul, Korea
- Marie Kranendonk-Schwartz, ANPED, Utrecht, Netherlands
- Ritu Kumar, UNIDO, Vienna, Austria
- Ing Hoc Lim, Ministry of Environment, Pnom Penh, Cambodia
- Alex Mc Gillavry, New Economics Foundation, London, UK
- Bedrich Moldan, Charles University, Prague, Czech Republic
- Chris Morrey and Andrew Randall, Department of the Environment, London, UK
- Bruce Nordman, Berkeley National Laboratory, California, USA
- Hans Opschoor, ISS, The Hague, Netherlands
- Kirit Parikh, Indira Ghandi Institute of Development Research, Bombay, India
- Istvan Pomazi, Chief Adviser Ministry for Environment and Regional Policy, Hungary
- Mark Radka, Industry Programme Officer, UNEP (Regional Office for Asia/Pacific), Bangkok, Thailand
- Jan Rotmans, International Centre for Integrative Studies (ICIS), Maastricht, Netherlands
- Bob Slater, Environment Canada, Ottawa, Canada
- Joachim H. Spangenberg, Wuppertal Institute for Climate, Kolomb, Germany
- Walter Stahel, Institut de la Duree, Geneva, Switzerland
- Patricia I. Vásquez, Fundación Ambiente y Recursos Naturales (FARN), and Industry Secretariat, Buenos Aires, Argentina
- Rosa Anna Weiss, Federal Ministry of Environment, Vienna, Austria
- Czeslaw Wieckowski, Director, Environmental Policy Department, Ministry of Environmental Protection, Natural Resources, and Forestry, Warsaw, Poland
- Keimpe Wierenga, European Environment Agency, Copenhagen, Denmark

Workshop participants:

1. Mr. Peter Bartelmus
Chief, Environment, Energy and Industry Statistics Branch
Statistics Division
Department of Economic and Social Affairs
United Nations
2, UN Plaza, room DC2-1650
New York, N.Y. 10017
United States
Tel: (1-212) 963 4581
Fax: (1-212) 963 0623
E-mail: bartelmus@un.org

2. Ms. Marie-Paule Benassi
Responsible, Sustainable Development Indicators
Environment Unit
Statistical Office of the European Communities
European Commission
Batiment Jean Monnet
L-2920 Luxembourg
Tel: (352) 4301 32297
Fax: (352) 4301 37316
E-mail: mariepaule.benassi@eurostat.cec.be

3. Ms. Ilze Blignaut
Environmental Officer, Department of Environmental Affairs and Tourism
Private Bag X 447
Pretoria 0001
South Africa
Tel: (27 12) 310 3437
Fax: (27 12) 322 6287
E-mail: bog_ib@ozone.pwv.gov.za

4. H.E. Carlston B. Boucher
Ambassador / Permanent Representative
Permanent Mission of Barbados to the United Nations
800 2nd Avenue, 2nd Floor
New York, NY 10017
United States
Tel: (1-212) 867 8431
Fax: (1-212) 986 1030
E-mail: cboucher@undp.org

5. Mr. Rae Kwon Chung
Counsellor
Permanent Mission of the Republic of Korea to the United Nations
866 United Nations Plaza, Suite 300
New York, NY 10017
United States
Tel: (1-212) 715 2229
Fax: (1-212) 371 8873
E-mail: n.a.

6. Mr. Peter Dearden
Environmental Economist
Department for International Development
94, Victoria Street
London SW1E 5JL
United Kingdom
Tel: (44 171) 917 0076
Fax: (44 171) 917 0679
E-mail: p-dearden@dfid.gtnet.gov.uk

7. Ms. Dianne Dillon-Ridgley (CHAIR)
Consultant
United States President's Council on Sustainable Development
2204 MacBride Dr.
52246-1722 Iowa City, Iowa
United States
Tel: (1-202) 408 5296
Fax: (1-202) 408 6839
E-mail: ddr@igc.org

8. Mr. Mats Ekenger
Head of Section
Ministry of the Environment
SE - 10333 Stockholm
Sweden
Tel: (+46 8) 405 22 43
Fax: (+46 8) 10 38 07
E-mail: mats.ekenger@environment.ministry.se

9. Ms. Sakiko Fukuda-Parr
Director
Human Development Report Office
United Nations Development Programme
Room 612, 304 East 45th Street
New York, NY 10017
United States
Tel: (1-212) 906 3600
Fax: (1-212) 906 3677
E-mail: sakiko.fukuda.parr@undp.org

10. Ms. Patty Goodwin
Board Member of the Global Action Plan United States
Broadstreet Productions
920 Broadway
12th Floor
New York, NY 10 001
United States
Tel: (1-212) 780 5700
Fax: (1-212) 780 5710
Email: pgoodwin@broadstreet.com

11. Mr. Theodore Heintz
U.S. Interagency Working Group on Sustainable Development Indicators
Assistant Director, Office of Policy Analysis
U.S. Department of the Interior
1849 C Street N-W
Washington DC 20240
United States
Tel: (1-202) 208 4939
Fax: (1-202) 208 5602
E-mail: theintz@ios.doi.gov

12. Ms. Hilary Hillier
Head of Environmental Statistics
Department of Environment, Transport and Regions
Floor 5/D12 Ashdown House
123 Victoria St.
London SW1E 6DE
United Kingdom
Tel: (44-171) 890 64 40
Fax: (44-171) 890 44 21
E-mail: hilary.hillier@nfp-gb.eionet.eu.int

13. Mr. Paul Hofseth
Special Advisor
Ministry of Environment of Norway
Myntgaten 2, P.O.Box 8013 DEP
N-0030 Oslo
Norway
Tel: (47) 22 245960
Fax: (47) 22 249561
E-mail: paul.hofseth@md.dep.no

14. Ms. Outi Honkatukia
Administrator
Country Studies and Environment Division
Directorate for Food, Agriculture and Fisheries
Organization for Economic Cooperation and Development
2 Rue Andre Pascal
75775 Paris Cedex 16
France
Tel: (33-1) 4524 7964
Fax: (33-1) 4524 1890
E-mail: outi.honkatukia@oecd.org

15. Mr. Eivind Hovden
Associate Expert
Program for Research and Documentation for a Sustainable Society (PROSUS)
Sognsveien 70
0855 Oslo
Norway
Tel: (47) 22 18 1070
Fax: (47) 22 18 2077
E-mail: eivind@prosus.nfr.no

16. Ms. Annette Hugo
Assistant Director, Sustainable Development
Department of Environmental Affairs and Tourism
Private Bag X 447
Pretoria 0001
South Africa
Tel: (27 12) 310 3446
Fax: (27 12) 322 6287
E-mail: omd_ah@ozone.pwv.gov.za

17. Ms. Maria Elena Hurtado
Director of global Policy and Campaigns
Consumers International
24 Highbury Crescent
London N5 IRX
United Kingdom
Tel: (44-171) 226 6663 ext.205
Fax: (44-171) 354 0607
E-mail: mhurtado@consint.org

18. Ms. Anne Kerr
Manager, Indicators and Assessment Office
Ecosystem Science Directorate
Environment Canada
9th Floor Place Vincent Massey
351 St. Joseph Boulevard
Hull, Quebec K1A OH3
Canada
Tel: (819) 994 9570
Fax: (819) 994 5738
E-mail anne.kerr@ec.gc.ca

19. Mr. Kotaro Kodawaki
Principal Strategic Planning Manager
Strategic Environmental Planning Division
Environment Agency, Prime Minister's Office
1-2-2 Kasumigaseki, 1 Chome, Chiyoda
Tokyo, Japan
Tel: (81) 3580 1704
Fax: (81) 3581 5951
E-mail: kotaro_kadowaki@eanet.go.jp

20. Mr. Bas de Leeuw
Sustainable Consumption and Cleaner Production Officer
UNEP Industry and Environment
United Nations Environment Programme
39-43 Quai Andre Citroen
75739 Paris Cedex 15
France
Tel: (33) 1 44 37 30 09
Fax: (33) 1 44 37 14 74
E-mail: bas.leeuw@unep.fr

21. Dr. Bedrich Moldan
Professor / Director
Charles University Environmental Center
Petrska 3
117 00 Praha 1
Czech Republic
Tel: (42-2) 2315334
Fax: (42 -2) 2315324
E-mail: bedrich.moldan@ruk.cuni.cz

22. Mr. Bruce Nordman
Research Associate
Lawrence Berkeley National Laboratory
University of California
Berkeley CA 94720 USA
United States
Tel: (1-510) 486 7089
Fax: (1-510) 486 4673
E-mail: bnordman@LBL.gov

23. Dr. Luiz Ramalho
Head of Section "Protection of the Environment and Natural Resources"
Carl Duisberg Foundation
Lützswufer 6-9
D-10785 Berlin
Federal Republic of Germany
Tel: (49 30) 25482 (0) - 100
Fax: (49 30) 25482 - 103
E-mail: ckamlage@e11.cdg.de

24. Mr. James M. Riordan
Director, National Office of Pollution Prevention
Environment Canada
351 St. Joseph Boulevard
Hull, Quebec K1A OH3
Canada
Tel: (819) 953 33 53
Fax: (819) 953 79 70
E-mail: james.riordan@ec.gc.ca

25. Ms. Barbara Schaefer
Economist
Federal Environmental Agency
FG I 4.2 - Department of Global Environmental Issues, Environment and Development
P.O. Box 33 00 22
D-14191 Berlin
Germany
Tel: (49) 30 8903 2149
Fax: (49) 30 8903 2920
E-mail: barbara.schaefer@uba.de

26. Ms. Carola Schmidt
Second Secretary
Permanent Mission of Germany to the United Nations
600 3rd Ave, 41st floor
New York, N.Y. 10016
Tel: (1-212) 856 62 87
Fax: (1-212) 856 62 80
E-mail: n.a.

27. Mr. Manfred Schneider
Councellor
Federal Ministry for Environment, Youth and Family
Stubenbastei 5
A-1010 Vienna
Austria
Tel: (43) 1 51522 1608
Fax: (43) 1 51522 7624
E-mail: manfreds@bmu.gv.at

28. Mr. Mahito Sei
Environmental Researcher
Strategic Environmental Planning Division
Planning and Coordination Bureau
Environment Agency, Prime Minister's Office
1-2-2 Kasumigaseki, Chiyoda
Tokyo, Japan
Tel: (81) 3580 1704
Fax: (81) 3581 5951
E-mail: masato_sei@eanet.go.jp

29. Mr. Joachim H. Spangenberg
Program Director, Sustainable Societies Program
Wuppertal Institute for Climate, Environment, and Energy
Doeppersberg 19
D 42 103 Wuppertal
Germany
Tel: (49) 202 2492 128
Fax: (49) 202 2492 138
E-mail: j.spangenberg@wupperinst.org

30. Ms. Julie Thompson
Department of Public Information
United Nations
Room S-1070 B
New York, NY 10017
United States
Tel: (1-212) 963 4295
Fax: (1-212) 963 6601
E-mail: Thompson2@un.org

31. Mr. Chris Tompkins
Department of Environment, Transport, and Regions (DETR)
Environment Protection International
Floor 4, Ashdown House
123 Victoria Street
London SW1E 6DE
United Kingdom
Tel: (44) 171 276 89 42
Fax: (44) 171 276 88 61
E-mail: ctompkins@epint.demon.co.uk

32. Ms. Anna Varkonyi
Commission on Sustainable Development
in Hungary
300 Winston Dr #1812
Cliffside Park, N.J. 07010
United States
Tel: (201) 224 21 61
E-mail: herald@compuserve.com

33. Mr. Herman Verheij
Directorate of International Environmental Affairs
Ministry of Housing, Spatial Planning and the Environment
Rijnstraat 8, P.O.Box 30945
2500 LG The Hague
Netherlands
Tel: (31-70) 339 48 70
Fax: (31-70) 339 13 06
Email: h.t. verheij@dimz.dgm.minvrom.nl

34. Mr. Jan Verschooten
Deputy Commissioner
Bureau Federal du Plan
Avenue des Arts 47-49
B-1000 Bruxelles
Belgium
Tel: (32-2) 507 7311
Fax: (32-2) 507 7373
E-mail: jav@plan.be

35. Ms. Minna Wilkki
Administrator
European Commission (DG XI.1)
Rue de La loi 200 (BU-5, 3/63)
B-1049 Brussels
Tel: (32) 2 299 5573
Fax: (32) 2 299 0895
E-mail: minna.wilkki@dg11.cec.be

DIVISION FOR SUSTAINABLE DEVELOPMENT
UNITED NATIONS DEPARTMENT OF ECONOMIC AND SOCIAL AFFAIRS

Division for Sustainable Development (DSD)
Department of Economic and Social Affairs (DESA)
United Nations
2, UN Plaza, DC 2 Building
New York, N.Y. 10017
United States

36. Mr. Kenneth G. Ruffing,
Officer-in-Charge
Room DC2210
Tel: (212) 963-0902
Fax: (212) 963-4260
E-mail: ruffing@un.org

37. Mr. Lowell Flanders
Assistant Director
Institutions, National Information and Major Groups Branch
Room DC2242
Tel: (212) 963-8809
Fax: (212) 963-1267
E-mail: flanders@un.org

38. Mr. Ralph Chipman
Senior Sustainable Development Officer
Socio-Economic Policies, Finance and Technology Branch
Room DC2214
Tel: (212) 963-5504
Fax: (212) 963-4260
E-mail: chipman@un.org

39. Mr. Erik Brandsma
Task Manager, Changing Consumption and Production Patterns
Socio-Economic Policies, Finance and Technology Branch
Room DC2286
Tel: (212) 963-0013
Fax: (212) 963-4260
E-mail: brandsma@un.org

40. Mr. Lars F. Mortensen
Consultant
Room DC2260
Tel: (212) 963-2137
Fax: (212) 963-4260
E-mail: mortensenl@un.org

41. Ms. Catherine Rubbens
Associate Expert, Socio-Economic Policies, Finance and Technology Branch
Room DC2288
Tel: (212) 963-5243
Fax: (212) 963-4260
E-mail: rubbens@un.org

42. Ms. Birgitte Bryld
Associate Expert, Institutions, National Information and Major Groups Branch
Room DC2254
Tel: (212) 963-8400
Fax: (212) 963-1267
E-mail: bryld@un.org

NOTES:

1. See Peter Hardi's contribution in: Moldan and Billharz, "Sustainability Indicators - Report of the Project on Indicators of Sustainable Development", 1997.

2. Commission on Sustainable Development, Fourth session, (18 April - 3 May 1996), "Changing Consumption and Production Patterns", Report of the Secretary-General, E/CN.17/1996/5.

3. In the "menu" (or core set) of indicators as included in the WPISD, indicators are grouped in categories covering the social, economic, environmental, and institutional aspects of sustainable development, and placed within a Driving Force-State-Response Framework. The indicators are also related to chapters of Agenda 21. More information about the WPISD is available on the internet (http://www.un.org/esa/sustdev/isd.htm).

4. For more information about the indicator framework used, reference is made to paragraph 3.1 of this paper.

5. The process was launched at a Workshop in Ghent, Belgium (20-22 November 1996): "Launching the Testing of Indicators of Sustainable Development". This Workshop was followed by a regional consultative meeting on Environmentally Sound and Sustainable Development Indicators in Bangkok, Thailand (26-29 November 1996), and two regional Workshops on Indicators for Sustainable Development: for Latin America and the Caribbean Region (San José, Costa Rica, 10-12 March 1997), and for Africa (Accra, Ghana, 3-6 June 1997). The fourth International Workshop on Indicators, hosted by the Government of the Czech Republic (Prague, 19-21 January 1998), brought countries involved in the national testing of indicators of sustainable development together, and allowed for exchange of experience and for the development of recommendations for improving the testing process.

6. Report of Expert Workshop on Methodologies for Indicators of Sustainable Development, (5-8 February 1996), Glen Cove, Long Island, New York.

7. Sustainable Consumption and Production, OECD, 1997. The term eco-efficiency was coined by the Business Council for Sustainable Development (BCSD) in "Changing Course", its report to the United Nations Conference on Environment and Development in Rio and discussed further at the OECD Workshop on Sustainable Consumption and Production in Rosendal, Norway, on 2-4 July 1995.

8. Sustainable Consumption and Production: Clarifying the Concepts, OECD, 1995.

9. The Carnoules Declaration, Factor 10 Club, Wuppertal Institute, 1994.

10. Factor Four - Doubling Wealth, Halving Resource Use, von Weizsäcker, Lovins, and Lovins, Earthscan Publications, 1997.

11. Programme for the Further implementation of Agenda 21, adopted by the Special Session of the General Assembly. See United Nations, General Assembly, Nineteenth special session, Overall Review and Appraisal of the Implementation of Agenda 21, A/S - 19/29, 27 June 1997.

12. Sustainable Consumption and Production, OECD, 1997, op.cit.

13. Sustainable Consumption and Production, OECD, 1997, op.cit.

14. Critical Trends - Global Change and Sustainable Development, UNDPCSD, DSD, 1997.

15. Potentials and Policy Implications of Energy and Material Efficiency Improvement, United Nations, 1997.

16. Critical Trends - Global Change and Sustainable Development, UNDPCSD, DSD, 1997, op.cit.

17. World Resources 1994 - 1995, A guide to the Global Environment, World Resources Institute, 1994.

18. Critical Trends - Global Change and Sustainable Development, UNDPCSD, DSD, 1997, op.cit.

19. Critical Trends - Global Change and Sustainable Development, UNDPCSD, DSD, 1997, op.cit.

20. The Best of Both Worlds - Lifestyles in the 21th Century, Ministry of Housing, Physical Planning, and the Environment, Netherlands, 1993.

21. OECD Environmental Data Compendium 1997 - Organization for Economic Cooperation and Development, Paris, France.

22. Calculations based on OECD Environmental data, Compendium 1997.

23. Changing Consumption Patterns in Human Settlements: Waste Management, UNCHS (Habitat) Settlement Infrastructure and Environment Programme (SIEP), 1997.

24. Resource Flows - the material basis of industrial economies, World Resources Institute, et. al, 1997.

25. I.e. the Netherlands Ministry of Housing, Physical Planning, and the Environment, and the National Institute for Environmental Studies, Japan.

26. Critical Trends - Global Change and Sustainable Development, UNDPCSD, DSD, 1997, op.cit.

27. Commission on Sustainable Development, E/CN.17/1996/5/Add.1.

28. Comprehensive Assessment of the Freshwater Resources of the World, World Meteorological Organization, et. al., 1997.

29. Comprehensive Assessment of the Freshwater Resources of the World, WMO, et. al., 1997, op.cit.

30. Commission on Sustainable Development, E/CN.17/1996/5/Add.1.

31. One participant of the consultative round proposed the following indicators, in order to indicate that ground and surface water use have different replenishment times: (I) surface water/total quantity of water use as a percentage of annual precipitation, or (ii) annual aquifer withdrawal as a percentage of replenishment.

32. See the Withdrawal/Availability ratios and the discussion with regard to water stressed countries in the "Comprehensive Assessment of the Freshwater Resources of the World", 1997.

33. The environment, space and living quality - time for sustainability, Margaretha de Boer, 1995.

34. Sustainable Consumption - A global perspective, Friends of the Earth Netherlands, 1996.

35. Critical Trends - Global Change and Sustainable Development, UNDPCSD, DSD, 1997, op.cit.

36. For underlying definitions, see World Resources (1996 - 1997), World Resources Institute.

37. International Institute for Sustainable Development, Unlocking Trade Opportunities - Case Studies of Export Success from Developing Countries, 1997.

38. The best of both worlds - Sustainability and quality lifestyles in the 21th Century, Ministry of Housing, Physical Planning, and the Environment of the Netherlands, 1993.

39. Calculations based on OECD Environmental data, Compendium 1997.

40. China Statistical Yearbook, 1995.

41. NCDO (Nationale Commissie voor Internationale Samenwerking en Duurzame Ontwikkeling), "Creatieve Democratie - Kroniek van Duurzaam Nederland", 1996.

42. Industrial Commodity Statistics 1993 Yearbook, Production and Consumption Statistics, United Nations, 1995.

43. TNO, Trendanalyse Consumptie en Milieu, 1996.

44. Many of the consumption trends discussed under other consumption clusters, such as food, mobility, and recreation, are also strongly affected by advertising.

45. Factor Four - Doubling wealth, Halving Resource Use, op.cit, and The Best of Both Worlds - Lifestyles in the 21th Century, op.cit.

46. Driving Eco-innovation - A breakthrough discipline for innovation and sustainability, Claude Fussler and Peter James, 1996.

47. More details can be found in "A Changing Future for Paper", World Business Council for Sustainable Development, 1996.

48. In 1992, buildings in industrialized countries consumed 58 per cent of total world buildings energy use, followed by developing countries (22 per cent) and economies in transition (20 per cent).

49. Potentials and Policy Implications of Energy and Material Efficiency Improvement, UNDPCSD, DSD, 1997, op.cit.

50. Potentials and Policy Implications of Energy and Material Efficiency Improvement, UNDPCSD, DSD, 1997, op.cit.

51. Potentials and Policy Implications of Energy and Material Efficiency Improvement, UNDPCSD, DSD, 1997, op.cit.

52. Potentials and Policy Implications of Energy and Material Efficiency Improvement, op.cit.

53. World Resources Institute, World Resources 1994-1995.

54. The Best of Both Worlds - Sustainability and quality lifestyles in the 21th Century, 1993, op.cit.

55. Unlocking Trade Opportunities, 1997, op.cit.

56. The Economist - A survey of travel and tourism, January 1998.

57. Unlocking Trade Opportunities, 1997, op. cit.

58. Unlocking Trade Opportunities, 1997, op. cit.

59. Environmental Indicators, OECD Core Set, 1994.

60. See Peter Hardi's contribution in: Moldan and Billharz, "Sustainability Indicators - Report of the Project on Indicators of Sustainable Development", 1997.

كيفية الحصول على منشورات الأمم المتحدة

يمكن الحصول على منشورات الأمم المتحدة من المكتبات ودور التوزيع في جميع أنحاء العالم . استعلم عنها من المكتبة التي تتعامل معها أو اكتب إلى : الأمم المتحدة ، قسم البيع في نيويورك أو في جنيف .

如何购取联合国出版物

联合国出版物在全世界各地的书店和经售处均有发售。请向书店询问或写信到纽约或日内瓦的联合国销售组。

HOW TO OBTAIN UNITED NATIONS PUBLICATIONS

United Nations publications may be obtained from bookstores and distributors throughout the world. Consult your bookstore or write to: United Nations, Sales Section, New York or Geneva.

COMMENT SE PROCURER LES PUBLICATIONS DES NATIONS UNIES

Les publications des Nations Unies sont en vente dans les librairies et les agences dépositaires du monde entier. Informez-vous auprès de votre libraire ou adressez-vous à : Nations Unies, Section des ventes, New York ou Genève.

КАК ПОЛУЧИТЬ ИЗДАНИЯ ОРГАНИЗАЦИИ ОБЪЕДИНЕННЫХ НАЦИЙ

Издания Организации Объединенных Наций можно купить в книжных магазинах и агентствах во всех районах мира. Наводите справки об изданиях в вашем книжном магазине или пишите по адресу: Организация Объединенных Наций, Секция по продаже изданий, Нью-Йорк или Женева.

COMO CONSEGUIR PUBLICACIONES DE LAS NACIONES UNIDAS

Las publicaciones de las Naciones Unidas están en venta en librerías y casas distribuidoras en todas partes del mundo. Consulte a su librero o diríjase a: Naciones Unidas, Sección de Ventas, Nueva York o Ginebra.

Litho in United Nations, New York
17898—July 1998—2,790
ISBN 92-1-104483-9

United Nations publication
Sales No. E.98.II.A.3